P9-DGH-023

THE ULTIMATE BOOK OF
WHISKEY

THE ULTIMATE BOOK OF
WHISKEY

OVER 200 SINGLE MALTS, BLENDS,
BOURBONS, AND RYES FROM AROUND THE WORLD

Joe Clark &
Stuart Derrick

PaRragon

Bath · New York · Cologne · Melbourne · Delhi
Hong Kong · Shenzhen · Singapore · Amsterdam

This edition published and distributed by
Parragon Books Ltd in 2015

Parragon Inc.
440 Park Avenue South, 13th Floor New
York, NY 10016
www.parragon.com

Written by Joe Clark
Feature text by Stuart Derrick
Designed by five-twentyfive.com
Project manager Tarda Davison-Aitkins
Production by Joe Xavier

ISBN 978-1-4723-6813-3

Printed in China

Joe Clark began working with whisky at the age of 20 in a specialist whiskey shop in his home town of York, after a short time his passion for the subject grew and he began to pursue a career in whisky. Now at the age of 27 Joe works for national whisky events company The Whisky Lounge and when not writing about whiskey can be found spreading its virtues far and wide in tutored tastings, whiskey festivals and whiskey schools all around the UK.

Stuart Derrick is a journalist, writer and editor with more than 20 years' experience writing for books, magazines, newspapers and organizations that need sparkling copy. He has written on subjects as diverse as travel, parenthood, corporate finance, marketing, motivation and broadcasting.

INTRODUCTION

18 SCOTLAND

122 IRELAND

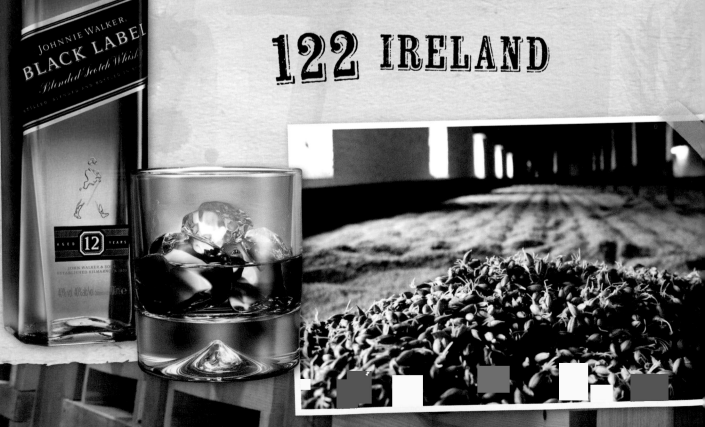

A SHORT HISTORY OF WHISKEY

Whiskey is the most popular dark spirit in the world. From its earliest incarnation as a locally produced drink for crofters and farmers in Scotland and Ireland, it has gone on to become a globally successful product, enjoyed by billions of drinkers.

The spirit is produced by distilling a fermented grain mash—typically, but not exclusively, malted barley—and the first written record of its production comes from Ireland in 1405. The Annals of Clonmacnoise, a seventeenth-century record of Irish history from ancient times until 1408, records the death of a chieftain as being due to "taking a surfeit of *aqua vitae*" at Christmas.

Aqua vitae, or "water of life," was the term used in the Middle Ages for distilled spirit. However, the process of distillation began thousands of years ago, possibly with the Babylonians in Mesopotamia as far back as 2000 BCE. The first clear evidence is provided by Greek alchemists in Alexandria in the first century CE, although this was not for the production of alcohol. By the tenth century Arab alchemists had discovered how to distill alcohol while making cosmetics. The word "alcohol" is derived from the Arabic *al-kuhl*, which means "the kohl": a type of eye makeup.

Although as Muslims the Arabs did not drink alcohol, they brought the knowledge of distilling to Europe, where it gradually spread through religious orders. Distillation of wine was recorded in thirteenth-century Italy, and medieval monasteries practiced the craft for medicinal purposes, treating ailments such as colic and smallpox.

Whisky production in Scotland seems to have been in operation by the late fifteenth century. An entry in the Exchequer Rolls for 1494 tells of malt being sent to a Friar John Cor "by order of the king, to make aquavitae." Cor was a monk at Lindores Abbey in Fife, and his royal connection to James IV required him to make around 1,500 bottles of the spirit for the king. This would not be the last time it enjoyed royal patronage.

Monks had distilled wine in some European countries, but as grapes were not readily available in Scotland, barley beer was distilled instead. Barley grew easily in the damp climate of Scotland, but those same conditions made it difficult to store. Beer making was one way of using barley and making it last. The processes of making beer and whiskey are very similar up to the point of distillation, and by distilling beer into spirit, a more potent brew could be created that lasted even longer.

The name derives from the Gaelic *usquebaugh*, which also means "water of life." Over time this phonetically became "usky" and finally "whisk(e)y."

Knowledge of distilling spread beyond the religious orders and became part of the farming year. It remained a cottage industry but was significant enough for the Scottish parliament to start taxing malt and whisky in the seventeenth century. Increasingly complex and inconsistent rates of taxation were applied following the Act of Union with England in 1707.

These taxes were widely seen as unfair and were accordingly flouted over the next 150 years, as excisemen, known as "gaugers," and smugglers tried

to outwit each other. Even ministers of the Kirk became involved, with some hiding barrels of whisky in their churches. Distillers looking to avoid the gaugers produced spirit at night, when darkness hid the smoke from the stills, giving rise to the nickname "moonshine."

The excisemen, who at one point included Scotland's national bard, Robert Burns, fought a losing battle. By the 1820s, as many as 14,000 illicit stills were confiscated every year, yet more than half of the liquor consumed in Scotland was still untaxed. In Edinburgh alone, there were eight legal stills in 1778, but an estimated 400 illegal ones.

Finally, a practical solution was proposed by the Duke of Gordon. In 1823 his Excise Act was passed, sanctioning the distilling of whisky in return for a license fee of £10, and a set payment per gallon distilled. The smugglers became legitimate almost overnight; many of today's distilleries date from the post-act period and are located on sites that were originally illegal stills.

Now that the producers were on a legal footing, the quality of the product could also be improved. This was aided by the adoption of the column still system, initially invented by Robert Stein at the Kilbagie Distillery in Clackmannanshire, and further refined by Irishman Aeneas Coffey. Also known as a continuous, patent, or Coffey still, it enabled the creation of lighter grain whiskies, which were more accessible and had a wider appeal. This revolutionized the industry in the 1840s and 1850s, as pioneering whisky blenders such as John Dewar, James Chivas, and George Ballantine were able to take light grain whiskies and blend them with heavier, peatier single malts from the pot stills.

Irish distillers produced their own version of whiskey, usually spelled with an "e" to distinguish it from Scotch. It was frequently smoother, due to being triple distilled and using less peat, and consequently found favor in both Britain and America.

However, Americans were also making their own whiskey by the late eighteenth century. Farmers found that it was a profitable way of converting surplus grain into a valuable product. As European malt did not flourish in America, they turned to corn and rye, producing distinctive American whiskey in the process. To the north, in Canada, distillers were making the same discovery and coming up with yet another twist on the formula.

Whiskey stole a march on other dark spirits, notably brandy, when the *Phylloxera vastatrix* vine louse devastated vineyards in France from the 1860s through to the 1880s. Until this point, brandy and soda had been the tipple of choice for the English middle classes. They now needed an alternative, and whiskey fitted the bill. Winston Churchill, who reputedly supped weak Johnnie Walker Black Label mixed with soda throughout the day, illustrated the generational change when he said: "My father could never have drunk whisky except when shooting on a moor or in some very dull, chilly place. He lived in the age of brandy and soda."

Since then whiskey has spread around the world, both as a drink and also as a product distilled in many different markets. While Scotch whisky maintains its claim on the spirit's heritage, whiskey is now a product of the world.

HOW SCOTCH WHISKY IS MADE

Whisky making produces an array of aromas, tastes, and colors, but they are all the result of a process followed by Scotch malt whisky makers using just three main ingredients: barley, water, and yeast.

MALTING

Barley is soaked in warm water and allowed to begin germinating for about a week. This turns the starch contained in the barley to soluble sugars, which are later converted to alcohol. A number of different barley varieties are used for single malt whisky, such as Golden Promise, Optic, and Chariot. The germination process is then halted by heating and drying. This "kilning" process is usually undertaken by drying the barley in a large oven. Traditionally these ovens were fed with peat, and this is what gives malt whisky its distinctive, smoky flavor.

MASHING

The dried malt is then ground in a mill and the resultant crushed "grist" is mixed with hot water in a mash tun, in a way similar to the process of making beer. Sugars in the malt are dissolved in the liquid, which is now known as "wort." The solid matter that is left over is often used as cattle feed.

FERMENTATION

The resulting wort is transferred to "washback" vessels, where yeast is added to allow fermentation and the creation of an alcoholic liquid called "wash." Different kinds of yeast, such as brewer's yeast and distiller's yeast, are added in varying combinations by expert distillers to influence both yield and quality. In Scottish distilleries it's all about yield and maximizing the alcohol from your barley, and as far as is known they all use distiller's yeast. American distillers, on the other hand, use different types and are very particular about yeast strains. The yeast converts the sugar in the wort to alcohol, resulting in a liquid that is about eight percent ABV.

DISTILLATION

The wash is then distilled twice, in copper wash stills. The stills are like large kettles where the wash is heated until it vaporizes and rises over the head of the wash still. The spirit is guided through condensers, which cool the vapor and return it to a liquid form in a second "spirit still," at which point it is known as "low wines." The process is then repeated in the spirit still in a slower form, with the liquid running into a locked spirit safe. There it is divided into three parts, based on alcohol quantity. The middle part is carefully extracted and stored in a spirit receiver, and this is the only part that becomes Scotch whisky. At this point tax is due to the United Kingdom government.

MATURATION

This clear spirit is known as "new make" and has an ABV of 60–75 percent. Most malt whisky is cut/diluted and filled into cask at 63.5 percent. It is now poured into oak casks for its long period of maturation. Legally it can't be called Scotch unless this period is at least three years (and is spent in Scotland). Many whiskies mature for much longer and acquire their distinct flavors and colors during this time. Scotch whisky may also have caramel coloring added prior to bottling, to give it a richer appearance. This is done to introduce a color consistency and is generally practiced by big brands and in blended whiskies.

Where a label carries an age statement such as "12-year-old" or "15-year-old malt whisky," all the whisky in the cask must have been matured for at least that amount of time.

GRAIN WHISKY

The process for making grain whisky is different. Grain is an essential ingredient of blended whisky, which has the lion's share of the market. It is therefore produced in huge quantities, and its production can seem a little more industrial than the more homespun approach of many malt whisky distilleries.

The mashing and fermentation processes are the same as those used for malt whisky, although only about ten percent of the mash recipe may be malted barley, with the bulk made up of wheat and corn. These grains are cooked prior to mashing to soften the grain starch and make it more soluble.

Grain whisky is then processed using a column still, which allows continuous distillation of spirit. This double column still has two components: an analyzer and a rectifier. The wash is pumped in at the top of the rectifier and flows down a coil, where it is warmed by the heat of vapors rising up the still. The wash then passes into the top of the analyzer, where it passes down through perforated plates. As it does so, steam rises up, extracting alcohol vapors and taking them back to the bottom of the rectifier. These vapors then start to rise and are gradually condensed by the cool wash coils and the grain spirit extracted from the column.

It may sound complicated, but the result is an extremely efficient process that creates grain spirit at around 94 percent ABV. This is then diluted to 68 percent ABV before being casked and matured, ready for the blending process.

WHISKEY OR WHISKY?

There are different types of whiskey around the world. Which is which?

SCOTCH WHISKY

According to the Scotch Whisky Association, Scotch whisky is a distilled spirit made in Scotland from cereals, water, and yeast. As the home of whisky, Scotland is very protective of its national drink, to the extent that the exact definition of "Scotch Whisky" has been enshrined in U.K. legislation since 1909, and recognized in European Community legislation since 1989.

The current U.K. legislation relating specifically to Scotch whisky is the Scotch Whisky Act 1988 and the regulations made under it in 2009, which govern the production, labeling, and presentation of Scotch. The regulations provide added legal protection for the traditional regional names associated with Scotch, such as "Highland," "Lowland," "Speyside," "Campbeltown," and "Islay." These can only appear on whiskies wholly distilled in those regions.

The regulations provide a detailed definition of what is Scotch whisky, the main points of which state that it has been:

- distilled at a distillery in Scotland from water and malted barley (to which only whole grains of other cereals may be added);
- distilled at an alcoholic strength by volume of less than 94.8 percent;
- matured only in oak casks of a capacity not exceeding 185 gallons (700 liters); and
- matured only in Scotland for at least three years.

Scotch whisky is divided into five categories:
- Single malt Scotch whisky;
- Single grain Scotch whisky;
- Blended Scotch whisky;
- Blended malt Scotch whisky;
- Blended grain Scotch whisky.

IRISH WHISKEY

The history of Irish whiskey runs parallel with that of its Scottish cousin, but the drinks are distinct. Apart from the fact that it is spelled with an "e," most Irish pot still whiskey is distilled three times, compared with twice for most Scotch. This results in a smoother taste, as does the fact that peat is rarely used in malting.

Irish whiskey was at one time more popular than Scotch, and some Scottish distilleries even tried to pass off their product as Irish. However, Irish whiskey experienced a long period of decline from the late nineteenth century onward, due to factors such as technological changes and the United States Prohibition laws. However, there has been a resurgence in Irish whiskey, and since 1990 a growth of about 20 percent per annum has resulted in the construction and expansion of distilleries.

Like Scotch, Irish whiskey is legally defined, in the Irish Whiskey Act of 1980. Primarily, it must be distilled and aged in Ireland for a period of at least three years.

AMERICAN WHISKEY

There are several types of whiskey made in America. Perhaps the best known is bourbon, an American whiskey produced in Kentucky, which must be made from a grain mixture of at least 51 percent and no more than 80 percent corn. The fermentation process for this mixture is often started by mixing in some mash from an older batch that is already fermenting: a process known as "sour mash." Bourbon can only be labeled as such if it has been made in the United States. The spirit must be distilled to no more than 80 percent ABV and aged in new charred oak barrels before being bottled at no less than 40 percent ABV.

Although bourbon has no minimum aging period, to call it "straight" bourbon, as with all "straight" whiskeys, it must be aged for not less than two years and can have no added coloring or flavoring.

Tennessee whiskey is made in the state of Tennessee using the Lincoln County Process, where the whiskey is put through a maple charcoal filter to improve the flavor. Because of this filtration it cannot be classified as a bourbon. Jack Daniel's is an example of a Tennessee whiskey.

American rye whiskey must be made with at least 51 percent rye in the mash, usually with corn and malted barley, and is aged in charred oak barrels. Rye whiskey was the prevalent whiskey of the northeastern states, especially Pennsylvania and Maryland, but largely disappeared after Prohibition. The predominance of rye gives what is described as a spicy or fruity flavor to the whiskey, and examples include Jim Beam.

Other types of American whiskey include corn whiskey, single barrel, and small batch.

CANADIAN WHISKY

Canadians opt for the Scottish spelling of whisky, and their take on the "water of life" must be distilled in Canada and aged for at least three years in oak casks. Like Scotch, it may contain caramel as a coloring agent. While it is often assumed that Canadian whisky is predominantly rye-based, legislation does not mandate what grain is used or in what quantities. Canadian distillers first started using rye as a flavoring agent to provide a tang to their spirit. While some whiskies do use rye, the primary grain used to make most Canadian whisky is corn, which is blended with rye grain whisky after distillation.

Unlike American straight whiskeys, in which the grain is blended in a "mash bill," or recipe, before fermentation, Canadian distillers generally do not use mash bills, but ferment and distill the individual grains separately, then blend them after distillation, or after they have matured in white oak barrels.

WORLD WHISKEYS

Whiskey or whisky is now produced in a bewildering array of countries not associated with traditional production. Some, such as Japan, actually have a heritage that goes back a surprisingly long way—the first distillery was founded at Yamazaki in 1923. Others, such as India, are emerging as huge producers in their own right to serve a vast internal market. The quality of the spirit is improving all the time, in countries from South Africa to Switzerland. Scotland's neighbor, England, is also getting in on the act with the Norfolk-based St. George's distillery, which has produced a range of lauded whiskies since 2006.

THE AGE OF THE BLEND

Following the introduction of Coffey's patent still in the mid-nineteenth century, distillers were able to produce huge amounts of fairly bland spirit rather cheaply.

Although some of this was drunk by poorer people in Scotland, the majority of it was sent to England to make gin. Most malt whisky was still drunk in Scotland.

The mixing of whiskies from different distilleries had been in practice for some time, and whisky was even mixed with herbs and other drinks to create a cheaper drink. In 1853, the Forbes-Mackenzie Act permitted the mixing of differently aged whiskies from the same distillery "under bond." This process, known as vatting, allowed distilleries to create more appealing and consistent blends of whisky.

One of the first distilleries to do so was Andrew Usher & Co., which that same year created Old Vatted Glenlivet, sometimes described as the first whisky brand. The 1860 Spirit Act opened the door farther to blends by permitting malts and grains to be blended under bond. These whiskies were cheaper to produce than malts, were more consistent, and had a much broader appeal.

Unlike malt whisky, grain whisky was produced using a new and far more efficient still, which created a much lighter style of spirit and allowed for far greater production. The new lighter grain whiskies were combined with the heavier malt whiskies, and in so doing the blended whisky was born.

Andrew Usher, who created Old Vatted Glenlivet, is sometimes seen as the father of blending. Usher's father, also called Andrew, had experimented with blending, but his son is widely regarded as having perfected the art. At the time, mellower Irish whiskey was gaining in popularity in Britain, and some Scottish distillers, such as Caledonian in Edinburgh, even started to create their own versions of it.

Usher's work in creating more balanced, lighter, and more drinkable whisky laid the foundations for Scotch whisky's growth over the next few decades. It also made him a fortune. By 1897 his North British Distillery was producing three million gallons of whisky a year and was the largest in Scotland. The previous year he donated £100,000 to build the Usher Hall concert venue in Scotland's capital, Edinburgh.

This period saw the development of many of the great blended Scotch whisky brands, such as Johnnie Walker, Dewar's, Black & White, Chivas Regal, Ballantine's, and VAT 69. Several other historical quirks combined to open up the market for Scotch whisky. The repeal of the Navigation Acts in 1849 created export opportunities for this new drink to Britain's colonies and dominions, where thirsty expats in Canada, India, New Zealand, South Africa, and Australia were desperate for a dram.

Blending whiskey is a considerable art acquired only after years of experience. A blend will consist of anything from 15 to 50 malt whiskeys and two or three grains. Whiskeys from different distilleries have a character of their own, and some whiskeys will not blend well with others. The blender's task is to combine different single whiskeys and produce a blend that brings out the best qualities of each of its constituent parts.

Every blend is different, not to mention secret, and the proportion of malt whiskey in each blend varies. It can be anything from 20–60 percent malt, and this will be reflected in the price.

The blender aims to produce a whiskey of recognizable character that will never vary from this consistent standard. This does not mean that the same whiskeys are used all the time or in the same proportions. The characteristics of the malts used will vary from year to year or may not be available at certain times, so the blender must ensure that the blend does not stray from the set formula.

Single whiskeys are brought from the warehouse to the blending establishment, where an experienced blender mixes them. The blender is looking at how the various whiskeys mix and the effect that has on the nose, the palate, and the finish. This is largely done through "nosing," or smelling, the whisky. After years of training, master blenders can tell a huge amount about a whiskey without it even reaching their taste buds.

Once the blend is created, the whiskey is usually returned to cask and left to marry for a period of months before bottling. However, some companies prefer to vat their malts and grains separately and only bring the two together before bottling.

Although blended whisky makes up the bulk of the Scotch whisky market, it has never quite had the

cachet attached to malt whisky, and is often seen as the poor relation. However, in recent years this has changed slightly, as specialist makers such as Compass Box have sought to create more upmarket blends in an artisan fashion, with price tags to match.

Blended whiskey has truly come of age.

THE SECRET'S IN THE OAK

One of the most important factors in making whiskey is time. It takes at least three years before new-make spirit can be called Scotch whisky, and is often left to mature for a lot longer.

Irish whiskey, Canadian whisky, and bourbon all have similar periods of maturation before they can be bottled.

The process of making and distilling the spirit is relatively quick—about a couple of weeks. After that the spirit is matured in a wooden barrel. Whiskey hardly changes once it has been bottled—all of the interesting alchemy takes place in a cask, usually of American white oak, *Quercus alba*. It is estimated that 60–80 percent of a whiskey's flavor can be attributed to what goes on in the barrel.

It is likely that the realization of the effect that barrel maturation had on whiskey occurred over time. In the nineteenth century, barrels were still used to store a range of dry and wet goods—everything from fish and butter to oil and beer. Reusing these barrels was a way for whiskey distillers to keep their costs down.

Through experimentation, distillers came to realize that oak barrels were best for storing whiskey. While being watertight, the barrels allow the liquid inside to breathe, helping to affect a change in its characteristics. The spirit that goes into the barrel at around 60–65 percent ABV is very different when it comes out a few years later.

This porosity is an important part of the process and results in some of the spirit—the so-called "angel's share," which can be up to two percent of volume a year—being lost during maturation. The wood in the cask also interacts with the spirit in a way that affects the flavor. Hemicellulose caramelizes, adding sweetness and color, while tannins produce astringency and fragrance.

A barrel is an incredibly complex construction, and the coopers who originally made them were skilled

artisans who underwent a lengthy apprenticeship of four or five years. Wet coopers were the most skillful, as their work had to prevent a precious load from leaking in the warehouse, where it was stored for years on end.

There are 20 million barrels of Scotch whisky in storage. Even in the heyday of coopering, the local industry and forests could not keep up with the demand since mature trees were needed. Instead it turned to reusing casks that had brought sherry, port, and Madeira into the docks of Britain. After the contents were bottled, the redundant casks were sold on to grateful distillers. What started as an exercise in parsimony became a valuable part of maturation, as distillers began to realize that the original contents beneficially mellowed maturing whiskey. These casks were hand coopered from European oak, *Quercus robur*, and served the whiskey industry for many years. However they were gradually superseded by bourbon barrels, which could be made more cheaply, as American oak, *Quercus alba*, lent itself to machining.

The American Standard Barrel (ASB) of 53 gallons (200 liters) is now widely used to store maturing whiskey. By law, American bourbon must be aged in virgin American oak barrels, after which they are surplus to requirements. For many years, they have been the first choice of Scotch whisky manufacturers. Some whiskies are still matured in sherry barrels, but they can cost ten times as much as a bourbon barrel.

The bourbon casks are broken down and shipped to Scotland, where skilled coopers reassemble them, sometimes adding extra staves to create the hogshead (66 gallons/250 liters). The barrels are often then fired on the inside. The resulting layer of active carbon removes some unwanted compounds in the liquor and increases the production of fruity lactones. Casks can be reused for about 70 years, with stripping and recharring in between fills.

Maturation in wooden casks also gives whiskey its golden color, as melanoidins from the breakdown of cellulose help to brown the spirit. Old sherry or rum casks can also darken the whiskey and contribute to its flavor. Caramel can be added to bring the whiskey to a standard color.

The size of a barrel also has an effect on maturation, as the inner surface area that the spirit reacts against varies. Distilleries with a high output, such as Glenfiddich or Glenmorangie, tend to use smaller barrels, since their whisky matures faster in these smaller cask types.

What goes on in the barrel remains something of a mystery to distillers, despite attempts to pin down the science. Bourbon distiller Buffalo Trace estimates that there are around 300 compounds in a barrel, and it has identified only 200 of them. The placing of a barrel in the warehouse can also have a profound effect on what the contents taste like, with barrels located near windows—so-called "honey barrels"—tasting better.

In recent years, the process of finishing whiskeys in particular barrels has also gained in popularity, with port, sherry, Madeira, and burgundy barrels used to impart a final flavor dimension to the whiskey. Once again, wood is the defining feature.

SCOTLAND

Scotch whisky is iconic, and has a proud place in the rich cultural heritage of Scotland. The country and the drink have become synonymous.

This is hardly surprising, as Scotland is known as the home of whisky. Its damp and cool climate may not always be welcoming, but it is ideal for producing two things that contribute to great whisky: barley and peat.

It is no longer the only place that you can get great whisky, and some people contend that the Irish may have beaten the Scots to the punch in distilling it. However, history is written by the winners, and it's hard to dispute that whisky has delivered this small country in Northern Europe a winning hand.

Exports of Scotch whisky were worth a record £4.3 billion in 2012, and contributed about £1 billion to the U.K. Exchequer in taxes. Scotch accounts for a quarter of U.K. food and drink exports, with 140 million cases exported worldwide to 200 different countries. A further 20 million casks lie maturing in warehouses in Scotland.

There are 108 distilleries licensed to produce Scotch whisky, employing 10,000 people directly and 35,000 indirectly across the United Kingdom. Whatever way you look at it, Scotch whisky is a massive success.

It's no surprise, then, that the description "Scotch whisky" is jealously guarded, and refers only to whisky that has been made and matured in Scotland under strictly defined conditions. Although Scotch whisky has been produced for hundreds of years, the actual definition of what constitutes Scotch is only just over a century old and dates back to a 1905 court case in Islington, London. The suit was brought by the local borough

council against two wine and spirit merchants for selling a "Fine Old Scotch Whisky" that was "not of the nature, substance, and quality demanded" by the provisions of the 1875 Sale of Food and Drugs Act. At a time when grain whisky was in the ascendant, the drink was composed of 90 percent grain and ten percent malt whisky.

Islington borough won the case, despite the merchants being supported by powerful distillers of grain spirit, but it led to a dissection of the question of what defined "whisky" by a royal commission. This reported in 1909 and determined that the term "Scotch whisky" covered malt, grain, and blended whisky.

Since then, Scotch whisky has been defined as a distilled spirit made in

Malt whisky was once an ultra-niche product and was not truly exploited until the 1970s and '80s, when distillers started to wake up to its potential. Their marketing worked so well that blended whisky suffered by comparison, becoming regarded as a kind of poor relation. In recent years this process has been reversed somewhat, with blended brands fighting back with new drinks that appeal to different—and inevitably upmarket—customers. Blended whisky now retains the vast share of volume sales.

Scotch whisky is divided into different regions: the Highlands, the Lowlands, Speyside, Islay, and Campbeltown. Each of the regions is said to produce whiskies with their own unique characteristics. For example, Lowlands whiskies such as Glenkinchie and Auchentoshan are generally held to be gentle and light, with a lack of the peatiness associated with other regions. By contrast, Islay malts, such as Bowmore and Laphroaig, have a peatiness and smokiness that make them quite distinct and something of an acquired taste.

These days it is sometimes debated whether such hard-and-fast definitions still hold true. Although the conditions in each region have historically helped

Scotland from cereals, water, and yeast. It must have been stored in Scotland in oak casks no larger than 185 gallons (700 liters) for a minimum of three years.

Adhering to these conditions, hundreds of Scotch whisky brands have developed. Blended Scotch such as Chivas Regal, Ballantine's, and Johnnie Walker are among the biggest spirit brands in the world. Malts such as Glenfiddich, Glenmorangie, and Highland Park have helped drive the market even farther. In the past 30 years they have targeted an aspirational group of drinkers who have readily embraced marketing laced with messages about connoisseurship and exclusivity.

Malts such as Glenfiddich, Glenmorangie, and Highland Park have helped drive the market even farther.

define the whiskies produced there, some feel there is now more of a blurring of the lines, as distillers seek to create new whiskies that appeal to modern drinkers.

Whatever the case, the future for Scotch whisky looks rosy, with continued demand leading to heavy investment in production. Only about 20 percent of Scotch whisky production is now in the hands of businesses from its country of origin, as major international players such as Diageo (Johnnie Walker, J&B, and Cardhu), Pernod Ricard (Ballantine's, Chivas Regal, and The Glenlivet) and Bacardi (Dewar's, William Lawson's, and Aberfeldy) dominate the market. The upside is that they are pouring billions into new and expanded facilities in Scotland, and have the marketing and distribution clout to make Scotch successful the world over.

At a lower level, the industry is also doing well, with new players emerging, often reinvesting in old distilleries and warehoused whisky. South African Billy Walker has bought a string of out-of-favor distilleries since 2004, putting The BenRiach, The GlenDronach, and Glenglassaugh back into the limelight.

Whatever the provenance of the producer, one thing is clear: the whisky is Scottish through and through.

SPEYSIDE

Speyside is a region spanning Morayshire and the Highlands area that is the heartland of Scotch whisky production. Its rich alluvial soils and Gulf Stream-aided climate raise excellent barley, and many mountainous hideaways made it a hotbed of illicit distilling in the past. Now that the industry is legitimate, it is home to around two thirds of the malt whisky distilleries in Scotland.

The first license to distill whisky legally in Scotland was granted in 1824 to George Smith and his son John Gordon Smith, of The Glenlivet distillery in Speyside. The Glenlivet style became so renowned that many distilleries adopted the name. Some were

so far away that it led to a joke that The Glenlivet must be the longest glen in Scotland. The Smiths eventually registered the name in London in 1870, but despite legal proceedings, the descriptor "Glenlivet" was used by other distilleries for many years afterward.

Broadly speaking, Speyside whiskies fall into two groups. At one end of the spectrum there are the light, grassy whiskies such as The Glenlivet. At the other end are rich, sweet, sherried whiskies such as The Macallan and Glenrothes. Generally, the Speyside whiskies use only minimally peated barley and tend to be lighter than other Highland and Island whiskies, although there are exceptions, such as The BenRiach and Ballantruan.

Speyside whiskies use only minimally peated barley and tend to be lighter than other Highland and Island whiskies.

However, there is no hard-and-fast rule as to the characteristics of Speyside whisky, and the style has altered over time. Although more than half of Scotland's distilleries are to be found in the region, the exact number is difficult to ascertain, as there is some dispute over whether some distilleries are Highland or Speyside. To add to the confusion, some distilleries that are usually thought of as Speyside declare themselves as Highland on their packaging: for example, The GlenDronach and anCnoc.

Certainly there are between 50 and 60 active distilleries. What is indisputable is that the region's distilleries are responsible for some of the world's best-selling whiskies, such as Glenfiddich, Glen Grant, and The Macallan.

Aberlour

Aberlour whisky sits comfortably within the top ten Scotch single malts sold worldwide. It is the most popular single malt in France—which is quite a claim, as France drinks more whisky than any other country in Europe. The whisky itself could be regarded as a more traditional style, as every release in its portfolio uses sherry casks to some extent in the maturation process. The range includes ten-, 12-, 16-, and 18-year-olds and also a small-batch cask-strength release called A'bunadh. The A'bunadh stands out in the range not only because it is bottled at cask strength, but also because it is aged entirely in oloroso sherry casks.

A'bunadh batch 42

Sherry-casked single malts don't get much bigger than this. Bold and spicy, with notes of dark chocolate, fruitcake, marzipan, and macerated fruit.

★ ABV: 60.3%
★ Type: Single Malt

Benrinnes

The Benrinnes distillery certainly isn't well known, and unless you're actively looking for this whisky you're pretty unlikely to come across it. The distillery is owned by Diageo but isn't under the spotlight like some of its other showpiece distilleries. Benrinnes is more of a trusty workhorse, toiling away in the shadow of Benrinnes mountain making a high quality and robust spirit, and adding the backbone to a handful of famous blends. As a result of being so camera-shy the core range only has one regular bottling, a 16-year-old from the Flora and Fauna series. Three other official bottlings have occurred in the past but have all been limited, the most recent of which was a cask-strength 12-year-old from a series called The Managers' Choice in 2010.

15-Year-Old

A strong and intense whisky with a more savory profile than other Speysiders, with notes of leather, pepper, and burned fruitcake.

★ ABV: 43% ★ Type: Single Malt

The Balvenie

The Balvenie distillery is unique among all the Scottish distilleries in that every stage of production can still be done on site. The distillery grows and malts its own barley, has its own coppersmith to maintain its stills, and even its own cooperage to build and maintain casks. The Balvenie is also one of the few family-owned distilleries left in Scotland and has remained under the ownership of William Grant & Sons since its construction in 1892. Since then The Balvenie has grown to be one of the most successful and well-known whiskies in the malt whisky world.

These days The Balvenie is capable of producing around 1.7 million gallons (6.4 million liters) of spirit and is among the top ten best-selling single malts worldwide. In 1996 The Balvenie was among the first distilleries to release a whisky finished in a port cask. This technique, although commonplace at many distilleries today, was groundbreaking at the time. Between The Balvenie and another well-known distillery, the concept of wood finishing grew and opened up the way for even more diversity and flavor within the malt whisky category.

The range has been chopped and changed in recent years but has now settled down after three new releases in 2012. The current range consists of 12 and 17 DoubleWood (aged partly in oloroso sherry casks), 12 and 15 Single Barrel, 21 PortWood, Thirty (30-Year-Old) and Forty (a 40-year-old). Travel retail releases can also be found, as well as a raft of limited releases, some of which have become sound investments and are very collectable. Discontinued releases include the Founder's Reserve Ten-Year-Old and the Signature 12-Year-Old.

Single Barrel 12-Year-Old

A soft honeyed whisky and a perfect example of Balvenie's house style. Notes of chocolate orange, freshly sawn oak, and cookie with a trace of coconut.

✴ ABV: 47.8% ✴ TYPE: Single Malt

DoubleWood 17-Year-Old

Sweet pastry studded with dates and raisins and drizzled with honey. Subtle waves of vanilla ice cream and jammy fruit appear in the background.

✴ ABV: 43% ✴ TYPE: Single Malt

The BenRiach

In 2004 new life was breathed into The BenRiach when the current owner (The BenRiach Distillery Co. Ltd.) bought the distillery from Chivas. Since the 1960s the distillery's sole purpose had been to make plenty of good malt whisky, peated and unpeated, to be used in any number of blends within the Chivas portfolio. But since the takeover the distillery has gone from strength to strength, and so has the whisky. The new owners acquired plenty of casks of aging stock in the deal with Chivas and quickly got to work on rebranding the whisky and bringing it into the twenty-first century, not only with a new look but also with a raft of new releases.

Experimentation began with different casks such as Madeira, rum, port, and wine for finishing. Casks of peated BenRiach, which were never to see the light of day, were recognized for their quality and in a radical step were bottled and sold as single malt. The result was stunning and now the distillery is one of only a handful championing peated whisky from Speyside and the mainland. The range consists of Heart of Speyside and The BenRiach 12, 16, 20, 25, and 30 Years Old. These releases are in the typical Speyside fashion, whereas Birnie Moss, Curiositas Ten-Year-Old, Septendecim 17-Year-Old, and Authenticus 25-Year-Old are all heavily peated. Aside from the core range, a plethora of peated and unpeated single cask and wood-finished releases can be found.

12-Year-Old

A sweet and delicate whisky and a great starting point for anyone new to Scotch. Notes of honey and vanilla combine with soft, fruity flavors.

★ ABV: 40% ★ TYPE: Single Malt

Curiositas Ten-Year-Old

Heavily peated but without the medicinal flavors sometimes found in peated whiskies. Traces of honey, mixed nuts, vanilla, and oaky spice twist and turn behind a veil of smoke and subtle peat.

★ ABV: 40% ★ TYPE: Single Malt

Benromach

Currently only producing around a quarter of its capacity, Benromach is undoubtedly Speyside's smallest distillery. The current owner, the family-owned Gordon & MacPhail, bought the distillery in a state of disrepair in 1993 and set to work on bringing it back up to speed. Gordon & MacPhail had long been an established independent blender and bottler, with a history reaching back to 1895, three years before this distillery was originally built. The current range consists of Traditional (no age statement or NAS), a ten-year-old and an annual cask-strength release. Benromach can also boast the first organic single malt, released in 2006. A collection of vintages, various wood finishes, and peated releases can also be found.

Organic

First released in 2006, this whisky was the world's first certified 100 percent organic whisky. A lively little whisky. Notes of lemon toffee and banana cake combine with punchy spice and a hint of tropical fruit.

✯ ABV: 43% ✯ TYPE: Single Malt

What does a whisky's age tell us?

For many whisky drinkers, the most important thing that they look at on a bottle, after the producer's name, is the age of the whisky. Is it an 8-year-old, or 12-, 15-, 25-, or even a 50-year-old?

Age has become synonymous with quality. The older the whisky, the more flavors it will will draw from the oak. This does not, however, always mean a better whisky. A whisky is only as good as the cask it is aged in and being 30, 40, or 50 years old does not guarantee its greatness. What it will guarantee is a high price.

All Scotch whisky must be matured for at least three years, and malts usually for a lot longer. The time spent in a cask is generally held to be the most defining aspect of a whisky's character. The spirit exchanges its initial unpleasant tang for a richer, more complex flavor profile, and this process continues for many years.

The age statement indicates the age of the youngest whisky in the bottle. Even single malts are mixed, with spirit from one year being mixed with that from another to maintain a consistent taste.

However, age doesn't always lead to excellence, and some markets, such as that in Italy, seem to have a preference for younger whiskies. There is also something of a move toward no age statement (NAS) whiskies, with The Macallan, Wild Turkey, Johnnie Walker, and The Dalmore going down this route. Partly this is due to a shortage of older whisky, which means that distillers have to put younger whisky on the market.

Cragganmore

The Cragganmore distillery was founded in 1869 during a boom period for Scotch and was well equipped to reap the rewards. Cleverly positioned to take advantage of new railroad lines, Cragganmore was able to receive raw materials and deliver its whisky by rail: a significant advantage over older distilleries of the period. This, combined with making a first-class spirit, secured Cragganmore's footing and made it a significant supplier of malt to James Watson & Co., which, at the time, was a major player in the industry and owned three other distilleries.

Over the decades Cragganmore has moved with the times and embraced modernization, expanding in 1901 and again in 1964. Some of the original quirks of the distillery, however, still remain, including its original flat-topped stills and worm tubs, still in use today. Cragganmore is now under the Diageo umbrella and provides malt for both White Horse and Old Parr blends. In 1988 the distillery was chosen to represent Speyside in Diageo's Classic Malts range. Since then the whisky has steadily grown in popularity and recognition.

As with all of the Classic Malts, Cragganmore has a very compact core range, with only a handful of limited releases ever emerging from the distillery. The core range includes a 12-year-old and a Distillers Edition finished in port pipes. Independent bottlings of Cragganmore can be found on occasion, although as with any of the classic malts these independent offerings can be scarce at best.

12-Year-Old

A smooth whisky aged in a combination of sherry and bourbon casks. Sweet and fruity with notes of buttery shortbread and orange zest and honey.

★ ABV: 40% ★ Type: Single Malt

2000 Port Wood Finish— The Distillers Edition

Released annually and matured partly in ex-port casks. Soft and sweet, with honey and cereal notes combined with a rich, red berry jam fruitiness.

★ ABV: 40% ★ Type: Single Malt

Cardhu

Few distilleries in Scotland have had such a smooth climb to success as Cardhu. Even in its humble beginnings as a simple husband-and-wife operation it seems demand outstripped supply. John Walker & Sons was so taken by the quality of Cardhu's whisky that it became an essential part of its blend and was the first distillery acquired by the company. To this day Cardhu's spirit is still highly sought after and remains an integral part of the Johnnie Walker blend. The vast majority of Cardhu's whisky is sold in Europe, mainly Spain, and for a long time the only way it could be purchased in the United Kingdom was by visiting the distillery. The core range includes 12-, 15-, and 18-year-olds and the Cask Reserve.

12-Year-Old

A classic Speysider: soft, easy-drinking whisky with a malty sweetness, notes of honeyed granola bar, vanilla, citrus, stewed apples, and toffee.

★ ABV: 43% ★ TYPE: Single Malt

WHAT THEY SAY ...

"I wish to live to 150 years old, but the day I die, I wish it to be with a cigarette in one hand and a glass of whiskey in the other."

—Ava Gardner

Dailuaine

Dailuaine is owned by Diageo and is one of the largest in the team, but out of all the whisky made at Dailuaine only around two percent goes into its own single malt bottling. The rest is destined to support the breadwinning brand of Diageo: Johnnie Walker. The distillery was founded back in 1852, and in 1889 became the first distillery in Scotland to build a pagoda-style roof. This was an experimental design, which was created to help draw smoke away more efficiently from the smoking lofts. The design was hailed a success and the pagoda roof became a familiar sight at many distilleries and part of the Scottish landscape. The core range from Dailuaine consists of only one bottling: a 16-year-old from the Flora and Fauna series.

16-Year-Old

An incredibly rich whisky aged in ex-sherry casks. Laden with rich, sweet, spicy dried fruit and spice with a touch of smoke.

★ ABV: 40% ★ TYPE: Single Malt

The GlenDronach

Rewind the clock to the 1970s and The GlenDronach was one of the top five best-selling single malts worldwide. But sadly, through a combination of closures, different owners, and neglect, the once well-known whisky regressed into the shadows of its competitors. After a steady decline the distillery was mothballed from 1996 until 2002, and operated for only a few years before closing again in 2005. This most recent closure was to change the distillery forever. Works were undertaken on the stills to convert them from an older method of direct firing with coal to a modern indirect method using steam coils. Before then they had been the last coal-fired stills operating in Scotland.

In 2008 the distillery started a new chapter. It was sold by Pernod Ricard (aka Chivas) to new and upcoming The BenRiach Distillery for £15 million. The new owner set about restoring the whisky to its former glory, and since the takeover has increased sales significantly, putting The GlenDronach back on the map for whisky drinkers around the globe.

The distillery has always been famous for producing a big, rich, sherry-casked style, but in more recent years some bourbon casks have been filled. However, investment to the tune of £5 million in sherry casks would suggest that the house style of The GlenDronach is secure and will remain intact. The core range from The GlenDronach includes a limited-edition Octarine 8-Year-Old, 12-Year-Old Original, Revival—15-Year-Old, Allardice—18-Year-Old, 21-Year-Old Parliament, and two wood finishes, Sauternes; and Tawny Port casks. As well as these core expressions, as with sister distillery The BenRiach, a collection of single-cask releases and experimental bottlings can be found.

12-Year-Old Original

A rich, warming whisky in the classic GlenDronach style, notes of dried fruits, caramel, vanilla, brown sugar, and cinnamon.

✷ ABV: 43% ✷ Type: Single Malt

Revival—15-Year-Old

The extra aging has delivered an even bigger, richer character. The classic sherry cask fruitcake flavors mingle with dark chocolate, juicy fruit, and hazelnuts.

✷ ABV: 46% ✷ Type: Single Malt

Glenfarclas

Glenfarclas is one of the few distilleries left that are still family-owned and have family members working within the business. The distillery has been in the Grant family (not the William Grant of The Balvenie/Glenfiddich) ownership for nearly 150 years, and despite numerous attempts by bigger companies to purchase the distillery, they remain fiercely independent. They uphold an unfaltering big, rich house style, very rarely stray from their traditional roots, and currently produce around 925,000 gallons (3.5 million liters) of spirit in some of the largest stills in Scotland. The distillery has long been famous for its heavily sherried house style of whisky. Only a small handful of distilleries are as committed to this style these days and even fewer deliver it as flawlessly. Two main types of sherry cask are filled at Glenfarclas, namely ex-oloroso and fino, both from Seville in Spain. But even with a very traditional style of whisky Glenfarclas is still capable of innovation, and in 1968 it was the first distillery to release a whisky commercially at cask strength.

The core range includes 10-, 15-, 21-, 25-, 30-, and 40-year-old expressions. There's also the 105 cask strength, a 17-year-old that is available in the United States and Japan, and an 18-year-old available in travel retail. Very few distilleries have a core range that can show off their spirit right through from ten- to 40-year-olds, with almost every age in between. But the range doesn't stop there, and Glenfarclas has another series called The Family Casks. The Family Casks series is unique and can show off some of the distillery's oldest whisky, with bottlings available from every year between 1952 and 1996, all bottled as single casks and at cask strength. Add to this range a string of anniversary bottlings and the occasional limited release, and you have the most incredible range of any distillery in the world.

This wealth of maturing stock is unique and you won't find this library of vintage bottlings from any other distillery. Independent bottlings have been available in the past but they aren't easy to come by, especially as they're usually under a different name and you won't find the word "Glenfarclas" anywhere on the label.

15-Year-Old

Soft and silky but not without a little bite. Notes of sweet, spicy fruit and butterscotch combine with red grape and a hint of peat.

✱ ABV: 43% ✱ Type: Single Malt

21-Year-Old

Soft and complex but with lighter flavors than the 15-year-old. Baked apples scattered with chocolate-covered raisins, vanilla, and gingerbread.

✱ ABV: 43% ✱ Type: Single Malt

105 Cask Strength

This whisky bursts with a fruity intensity that almost knocks you back. As it holds on to your palate, it grows with sweetness and delivers an explosion of grapy fruit and spice along with light treacle.

✱ ABV: 60% ✱ Type: Single Malt

Glenfiddich

Glenfiddich is the best-selling single malt worldwide and has sat at the number-one spot for many years now. The distillery dwarfs its neighbors and operates traditional equipment on an industrial scale. Two mash tuns, each capable of holding 11.5 tons of grist, a jaw-dropping total of 24 washbacks, and 28 stills combine to create an annual production of an incredible 2.65 million gallons (10 million liters) of spirit a year.

This success didn't happen overnight, of course, and has been building since the distillery was founded in 1887. A combination of innovative ideas, a clever strategy, and a good product have earned Glenfiddich the top spot. The most groundbreaking of its ideas came in 1963, when Glenfiddich became the first distillery to market its whisky as a single malt. It might seem odd that a distillery would wait 77 years after its founding before bottling and selling its own single malt. But up until this point distilleries had made a living by selling their whisky to blenders and bottlers, the most successful of which have grown into the big brands we know today.

This bold move soon paid off and in 1969 Glenfiddich claimed another first when it opened the first distillery visitor center. It didn't take long for other distilleries to catch on and follow in its footsteps, forever changing the way whisky would be perceived, sold, and consumed.

To this day the distillery remains under the ownership of its founders, William Grant & Sons. Sister distillery The Balvenie and the famous Grant's blend are also under the same banner. The core range includes 12-, 15- (Solera Vat), 18-, and 21-year-olds (Gran Reserva, finished in rum casks), also a 15-year-old Distillery Edition. Older expressions have included 30-, 40-, and 50-year-olds. Travel retail releases are also available, most recently a wood-finished series called Age of Discovery. A raft of limited and commemorative bottlings has been released over the years, some of which have become very collectible and can reach high prices at auction.

12-Year-Old

The classic 12-year-old, easygoing, sweet, and fruity, this whisky is perfect for recruiting single malt whisky drinkers the world over.

✴ ABV: 40% ✴ TYPE: Single Malt

Distillery Edition (15-Year-Old)

Bottled at higher strength, this Glenfiddich has more grip and bags more flavor. Subtle floral notes evolve into dark fruit flavors, pepper, and oaky spice.

✴ ABV: 51% ✴ TYPE: Single Malt

21-Year-Old

This release is aged primarily in American oak casks and then finished in rum casks for around four months. The resulting whisky is deep, rich, and complex, with notes of honeysuckle, figs, sticky toffee pudding, and rum-and-raisin ice cream.

✴ ABV: 43% ✴ TYPE: Single Malt

The World's Leading Malt

The eponymous whisky takes its name from Glen Fiddich, or "valley of the deer," where its Dufftown distillery is located. The stag on its logo is a canny reminder of the location.

Since being established by William Grant in 1887, the Glenfiddich distillery has grown to become Scotland's largest producer of single malt whisky, with a capacity of 2.65 million gallons (10 million liters) of alcohol per year. It is generally held to be the world's best-selling single malt, accounting for one in seven bottles of malt whisky bought worldwide in 2007.

Whatever its position in terms of sales, Glenfiddich can claim to have set the bandwagon rolling on malt whisky's revival. The family firm has always had a knack for marketing, as evidenced by a world sales tour in 1909 by William Grant's son-in-law, Charles Gordon. It also introduced the revolutionary triangular bottle designed by Hans Schleger in 1961, and was the first distillery to introduce a tour.

In 1963 it set about marketing malt whisky internationally to a world that thought that blended whisky was the be-all-and-end-all. By recognizing the importance of new channels such as duty free, the company got a head start that it has never relinquished.

Today, Inspector Morse's favourite tipple is available in many expressions, including the classic 12- and 15-year-olds.

Glen Grant

Glen Grant is a big hitter in Europe, particularly in Italy, where it has claimed the number-one spot for best-selling single malt for many years. In its early years Glen Grant was regarded as an industry innovator, being one of the first distilleries to bottle its own whisky. These days it is less innovative, but its young and well-priced official bottlings serve as a great introduction to whisky, while older independent bottlings receive admiration and high praise from whisky specialists around the globe. The distillery matures mostly in American oak casks, but some sherry butts are used. The core range consists of The Major's Reserve (an NAS bottling), ten- and 16-year-olds, and a five-year-old bottling for the Italian market.

Ten-Year-Old

A light, clean dram with plenty of vanilla and a fruity character. Slightly nutty with a decent spicy finish.

★ ABV: 40% ★ Type: Single Malt

Glenlossie

For as long as Glenlossie has been making whisky it has been highly sought after by blenders to be used in a number of whiskies. This remains true to this day, with the bulk of whisky made at Glenlossie being used by the well-known brand Haig. Because of its popularity as a blending malt, Glenlossie has always been elusive in single malt form, which is understandable when around 99 percent of all the spirit made is used for blending. The first official bottling of Glenlossie was released in 1990 as a ten-year-old in the Flora and Fauna series and is still the only regular release available. Fortunately numerous independent bottlings can be found.

Berry Brothers Glenlossie 1992 20-Year-Old Cask No 3464

A sweet, cakey-style whisky. Candied and sweet with oaky spice and vanilla custard wrapped up in a soft, creamy mouthfeel.

★ ABV: 46% ★ Type: Single Malt

WHAT THEY SAY ...

"There are two things a Highlander likes naked, and one of them is malt whisky."

—Scottish proverb

The Glenlivet

The Glenlivet is among the best-known single malt whiskies and is available across the world. The distillery was founded in 1824 and is one of the biggest malt whisky distilleries in Speyside, producing 2.65 million gallons (10 million liters) of spirit a year, similar in scale to Glenfiddich.

The year 1824 was a turbulent one in the history of whisky production and saw many illicit distillers shut down. The Excise Act of the previous year had made it easier and cheaper to acquire a license to produce whisky legally, but The Glenlivet was one of the only distilleries to do this. As a result the owner, George Smith, became very unpopular among his neighbors in the valley, receiving numerous threats to burn his distillery and also on his own life. The threats were very real and for years George carried two pistols on him day and night.

The range features the 12-Year-Old, the 15-Year-Old French Oak Reserve, 18- and 21-year-olds, and The Glenlivet XXV. This main range is complemented by a non-chill-filtered range called Nàdurra, which features a 16-Year-Old at cask strength, a 16-year-old 48 percent (for travel retail), and the Nàdurra 1991 Triumph. Aside from these, a string of other exclusive releases can be found in travel retail and in many countries, for example a 12-year-old bottling called Excellence can only be found in Hong Kong. Some incredibly old bottlings can also be found in the Cellar Collection, which was released in 2012.

12-Year-Old

Incredibly light, soft, and easy drinking. A fantastic entry level malt with notes of honey, ripe green fruit, and vanilla.

★ ABV: 40% ★ Type: Single Malt

Nàdurra 16-Year-Old

Honey, vanilla, and sweet spices appear on the nose, with fruit and honey on the palate leading to a long, sweet, spicy finish.

★ ABV: 55.5% ★ Type: Single Malt

The Glenrothes

The Glenrothes distillery was founded by James Stuart in 1878, and began producing spirit in 1879, with the stills beginning to flow on the very same day that a terrible train accident occurred in Scotland. The Tay Bridge collapsed, plunging a passenger train into icy water, and taking at least 59 people to their deaths. After a few years James Stuart left the business, leaving his business partners under financial pressure. But for the next four decades the distillery enjoyed relative success, expanding production with the addition of new stills in 1896, and benefiting under the management of experienced Speyside distiller John Smith.

In 1922 the distillery suffered its first major disaster when a fire swept through one of the warehouses, destroying 200,000 gallons (909,200 liters) of maturing whisky. Fortunately, the following year a long-term relationship was formed with Berry Bros. & Rudd, which in 1923 created the Cutty Sark blend in which The Glenrothes spirit would play a significant role.

As sales of the blend grew, so did The Glenrothes, expanding several times in order to meet demand. By 1989 the distillery was operating ten stills, which boosted capacity to an impressive 1.7 million gallons (5.6 million liters). In 1994 The Glenrothes became one of the first distilleries to do away with age statements and began to bottle its single malts as vintages. Many have been released over the years in varying quantities. The standard bottling is released under the name Select Reserve, and is currently followed by 1998, 1995 and 1988 vintages, with many other expressions available. Today the brand is owned by Berry Bros. & Rudd, but the distillery is under the ownership of Edrington, which also acquired the Cutty Sark brand.

Select Reserve

....

Soft and fruity on the nose, with vanilla and soft fruit on the palate leading to a sweet, long finish.

✴ ABV: 43% ✴ TYPE: Single Malt

1998 Vintage

....

Soft and very approachable whisky. Rich, spicy fruit on the nose, with citrus, toffee, and vanilla on the palate and finish.

✴ ABV: 43% ✴ TYPE: Single Malt

Knockando

As with many malts from the Diageo stable, Knockando has a particular focus on a specific market: in this case France and Spain, where the brand enjoys relative fame. Aside from being a popular single malt in Europe, Knockando is a key blending malt for J&B, a popular blend found worldwide. For a distillery that enjoys relative fame it's unusual that it has no visitor center and is closed to the public. Mainly American oak casks are used for maturation but some sherry butts are also filled. The core range includes a 12-, 15-, 18-, and a 21-year-old. Only a handful of limited releases have made it out of Knockando, and independent bottlings can be very tricky to find.

12-Year-Old

A typical Speysider with a light body and a honeyed, nutty character. A great introduction to the Speyside style.

✯ ABV: 43% ✯ TYPE: Single Malt

WHAT THEY SAY …

"We borrowed golf from Scotland as we borrowed whiskey. Not because it is Scottish, but because it is good."

——Horace Hutchinson

Linkwood

Linkwood has been chopped and changed numerous times over the decades by various owners in order to satisfy a growing demand for its whisky. From these various expansions and refurbishments a giant distillery has emerged, which is now capable of extremely efficient whisky production. Despite its size, official bottlings from Linkwood are fairly scarce, with the only consistent release being a 12-year-old in the Flora and Fauna series. Fortunately, you don't have to look too far to find an independent bottling. Gordon & MacPhail has bottled a 15-year-old for a number of years and most indie bottlers will have bottled a Linkwood at some point. Being a relatively unknown whisky, older independent bottlings can be very good value.

Flora and Fauna 12-Year-Old

A light, sweet, and delicate whisky, its aroma is dominated by floral notes and prominent citrus evolving into lemon toffee and a slightly nutty character.

✯ ABV: 43% ✯ TYPE: Single Malt

Longmorn

Longmorn whisky isn't the easiest to find, and unless you visit out-of-stock whisky specialists on a regular basis you're unlikely to come across it. Longmorn is currently under the ownership of Chivas (Pernod Ricard) and certainly isn't given the same attention as other brands in the portfolio. With Glenlivet playing the leading role and Aberlour playing second fiddle, there's very little spotlight left for Longmorn.

However, if you start looking for this whisky you will find it, and many would say that it is time well spent. Longmorn is a more substantial Speyside whisky, with a heavier mouthfeel and generally more backbone than some of the better-known and easy-drinking brands. Longmorn's whisky has always been highly regarded by blenders and forms an intrinsic part of many blends, notably Chivas Regal and the more premium Royal Salute, often seen in travel retail. Thanks to its high demand among blenders, Longmorn generally operates under the radar of most whisky drinkers, with only a small amount making it out as a single malt. The distillery stands within a stone's throw of the The BenRiach distillery, and they were both founded by John Duff. But Longmorn, unlike BenRiach, is not open to the public, although occasional open days have occurred. Only one official bottling of Longmorn can be found, a 16-year-old, which replaced a 15-year-old around 2007. Thankfully many independent bottlings of Longmorn can be found; the second featured here was bottled by Douglas Laing, who bottle their whiskies as single casks. Unlike a regular distillery bottling, in which many casks are brought together to create a consistent product, single-cask whiskies offer a one-off snapshot of the distillery in question.

16-Year-Old

Buttery and rich, with creamy toffee, honey, sweet spicy fruit, and traces of oaky spice in the finish.

✴ ABV: 48% ✴ Type: Single Malt

1991, 21-Year-Old, Old Malt Cask, #8256

A very different creature to the 16-Year-Old. Sweet cereal notes on the nose, with subtle citrus, toffee, and cinnamon.

✴ ABV: 50% ✴ Type: Single Malt

The Macallan

The Macallan distillery is one of Speyside's largest and best-known distilleries, with a huge following around the globe. The brand has done an excellent job over the decades expanding itself as a premium luxury whisky, with the term "The Rolls Royce of Whisky" often used by fans. The whisky has long sat in the top five best-selling single malts, but in recent years has been neck and neck with The Glenlivet, fighting for second place behind Glenfiddich. The Macallan is a good starting point for many people new to whisky, as it is noticeably softer and more approachable than others, and depending on which release you pick up, it can also be a great example of sherry casking, too.

The distillery has always placed a heavy emphasis on the quality of its production methods, and unusually for a large distillery has tiny, short, fat stills, 14 of which can be found in two separate stillhouses working hard to create 2.65 million gallons (nearly ten million liters) of new-make spirit a year. Like Glenfarclas and The GlenDronach, The Macallan are advocates of the sherry cask, investing millions of pounds in their wood management. For many years only sherry cask expressions of The Macallan were available, but with the addition of the Fine Oak range in 2004 fans were able to see The Macallan in a new light. The Fine Oak range utilizes both American oak casks and sherry casks, which results in a much lighter style than earlier expressions.

The range from The Macallan is enormous and includes the Sherry Oak range, which features 12-, 18-, 25-, and 30-year-olds; these are the traditional 100 percent sherry-matured bottlings. The Fine Oak range features 10-, 12-, 15-, 17-, 18-, 21-, 25-, and 30-year-olds, and as above uses both sherry and bourbon casks. The 1824 series is the latest range from The Macallan and was launched in 2013. It features four expressions called Gold, Amber, Sienna, and Ruby. These releases were a bold move from The Macallan, as they are their first releases with no age statements. Beyond these ranges is a library of vintages and limited/commemorative releases. The Macallan can also boast some of the highest price tags found in the world of whisky, with some incredibly old releases selling for hundreds of thousands of pounds. Indeed, at the time of writing, The Macallan holds the record for the most expensive single malt ever sold.

12-Year-Old

Soft, creamy, and mouth coating, with notes of soft fruit and cocoa on the nose and palate building to a long, dry, spicy finish.

★ ABV: 40% ★ Type: Single Malt

18-Year-Old

Deep, dark and complex with intense fruit and spice on the nose. Soft and chewable with more rich fruit and dark chocolate flavors on the palate and spicy oak on the finish.

★ ABV: 40% ★ Type: Single Malt

The Macallan Ruby

A more delicate nose of dried fruit and raspberry cheesecake, with summer fruit pudding and ginger on the palate and oaky spice on the finish.

★ ABV: 43% ★ Type: Single Malt

Peat's place

Peat is an essential component in some Scotch whiskies, especially those from the Highlands and Islands. This traditional source of free fuel is used to bring a smoky flavor to whiskies such as Lagavulin, Ardbeg, and Laphroaig.

Although peat fires would once have dried the barley, these days peat "reek" is used more sparingly as a source of flavor. Peating times vary from 16 to 24 hours, after which the grain will not absorb any more flavor. It is then dried to reduce the moisture content.

Different peats produce different flavors: for example, peat from near the sea contains more seaweed and sand than moorland peat, which has more moss and heather.

Traditionally, many distilleries had their own maltings, indicated by pagoda-shaped chimneys that helped to disperse the peat smoke more effectively. Today only a few distilleries still malt their own barley using peat. These include Highland Park, Springbank, Bowmore, Laphroaig, and Kilchoman. Others use commercial maltings such as Islay's Port Ellen.

Peatiness is measured in part per million (PPM) of phenols, the compounds that provide the smokiness in whisky. Heavily peated single malts have a PPM of more than 30: for example, the highly peated Ardbeg and the Octomore of Bruichladdich score 50 PPM and 80 PPM respectively. Medium-peated is around 20 PPM, and lightly peated below 15 PPM.

Mannochmore

Mannochmore was one of a handful of distilleries to be built in the early 1970s, before a notable crash in the Scotch whisky market caused by overproduction in the industry. This period of bust saw many distilleries close and lasted from the mid-1970s through to the early 1990s. Although the distillery survived this downturn, it was mothballed for a number of years. It was silent in the years 1985–89 and then again between 1995–97. Despite being built in a turbulent time for whisky, the distillery has been a relative success for its owners and has kept on chugging away making whisky for some well-known blends such as Dimple. The only regular bottling to be found is a 12-year-old in the Flora and Fauna range.

12-Year-Old, Flora and Fauna

A gentle and delicate whisky with a soft character, floral notes, and a sweet, buttery, cakey feel.

★ ABV: 43% ★ TYPE: Single Malt

Mortlach

The future for the Mortlach distillery is looking bright, as owner Diageo has taken the plunge and aims to establish the distillery as a bigger player in the malt whisky category. As Mortlach is one of the main contributing malts to Johnnie Walker Black Label, this decision can't have been made lightly, and it comes at the same time as an £18 million (U.S.$30 million) investment in expansion of the distillery, after which its output will have roughly doubled. A new stillhouse with exact replica stills is planned, capable of mirroring the unusual distillation method, so that Mortlach should, in theory, create the same spirit. Until the new range planned for summer 2014 is released, the core range consists only of a 16-year-old in the Flora and Fauna series.

16-Year-Old, Flora and Fauna

Sometimes known as "The Beast of Dufftown." A heavily sherried style and a cult classic. Deep, dark, fruity flavors weave around ripples of smoke in this complex and charming whisky.

★ ABV: 40% ★ TYPE: Single Malt

Strathisla

Strathisla is one of the oldest distilleries in Scotland and one of the most scenic, attracting thousands of visitors from around the world each year. The distillery has long been known as the Home of Chivas and has been under its ownership since 1950. Through the success of the Chivas blends worldwide, the vast majority of Strathisla's spirit is already accounted for. As a direct result, the core range from Strathisla is very small and consists of only two bottlings: a 16-year-old cask-strength release that can only be found at the distillery, and a 12-year-old (revamped in early 2013). Independent bottlings can be scarce but have occurred, mainly from Gordon & MacPhail and occasionally from Douglas Laing.

12-Year-Old

Soft and approachable, with notes of stewed fruit, chocolate, toffee, gingerbread, and honey.

★ ABV: 40% ★ Type: Single Malt

Tamnavulin

Tamnavulin is a modern distillery and was built to meet a growing demand for malt whisky for blenders in the 1960s. At its conception it was owned by Invergordon Distillers Ltd., which became part of Whyte and Mackay in 1993. Shortly after this takeover, in 1995, the distillery was mothballed and remained silent until 2007, when it was reopened. Almost every drop of Tamnavulin makes its way into Whyte and Mackay's blending program, with only a tiny percentage ever having been bottled as a single malt. However, when expressions are found it can be a very rewarding dram. The only official bottling released was a 12-year-old, which has now been discontinued. Although this whisky may seem almost impossible to find, it can be found under another guise as Ben Bracken, a single malt mainly found in supermarkets.

12-Year-Old

A light and delicate whisky with delicate floral notes combining with a malty sweetness, ripe fruits, and a trace of smoke.

★ ABV: 40% ★ Type: Single Malt

Tomintoul

Tomintoul is one of only a handful of independently owned distilleries left in Scotland. Angus Dundee Distillers acquired the distillery from Whyte and Mackay in 2000, and since then have guided the distillery down a more innovative track. The main priority of the company is to continue to produce and export its wide portfolio blend, but it has certainly given Tomintoul a push into the spotlight. Since 2000 Tomintoul has released around 20 different expressions, but the core range now includes 10-, 14-, 16-, 21-, and 33-year-olds backed up with two peated releases: Peaty Tang and Old Balluntruan. Some limited releases can be found, including two 12-year-olds from port and sherry casks. In May 2013 they also released their first single-cask bottling: a 31-year-old. Independent bottlings can also be found.

16-Year-Old

An easygoing and well-rounded whisky, with notes of lemon meringue pie, caramel, honey, vanilla, and granola bars.

★ ABV: 40% ★ Type: Single Malt

Tormore

The Tormore distillery certainly stands out from the crowd of distilleries in Speyside. Built in 1958–60, the striking design seems to reflect the aspirations of the owner, who was hoping to take advantage of the boom period that followed World War II. This unmistakable distillery, however, hasn't released many (if any) expressions to attract the whisky enthusiasts, and like many of its neighbors is focused on supplying any number of blends with malt whisky. The core range stands at a 12-year-old from 2004, which replaced a ten-year-old available through the 1990s. Independent bottlings have been more numerous in the last few years and have been appearing from Signatory, Douglas Laing, and Berry Bros., to name but a few. The distillery matures its spirit almost entirely in American oak, but the occasional sherry cask is filled.

12-Year-Old

A mild whisky with a creamy texture, caramel, mint, lemon loaf cake, toasted almonds, and subtle spice.

★ ABV: 40% ★ Type: Single Malt

LOWLANDS

Lowland whiskies were once predominantly used as a source for blending in Scotland, and by the late nineteenth century most production was for this purpose. The area has little or no peat, so its whisky is much lighter in style than that of other regions.

Because of their light, easy-drinking character, the whiskies in the area are sometimes known as the "Lowland Ladies." As well as being light in body and aroma, this feminine character shows itself in a fresh, grassy, and lemony nature, with flavor that may begin sweet but rapidly becomes dry.

Whereas in most of the whisky regions there can be a blurring of lines in how a style tastes, Lowland whiskies are quite singular. As well as the lack of peat and salinity, this can be accounted for by the triple distillation of some Lowland whisky, notably Auchentoshan, producing a very smooth drink.

Although there were once many distilleries in the Lowlands and Borders, their numbers declined as Highland and Speyside whiskies became more popular. Today there are five malt whisky distilleries operating in the Lowlands. Auchentoshan, Glenkinchie, and Bladnoch are the better known, and

The area has little or no peat, so its whisky is much lighter in style than that of other regions.

their ranges include at least one typical Lowland malt expression.

Three new Lowland distilleries have planned production in recent years, although none has yet brought a product to market. Ailsa Bay, sited at William Grant & Sons' Girvan distillery, and Daftmill, a microdistillery based on a working farm in Fife,

have already distilled spirit. Another project to revive the Annandale distillery, which closed in 1919, began distilling in April 2014 and will eventually employ approximately 20 people.

Lowland whisky from four closed distilleries can also still be found. Rosebank, which was mothballed by United Distillers in 1993, is generally considered to be the best Lowland malt. More rarely seen are St. Magdalene from Linlithgow, Littlemill from Bowling, Dumbartonshire, and Ladyburn, from Girvan.

Auchentoshan

The Auchentoshan distillery is sited on the banks of the River Clyde, just outside Glasgow, and was granted its license to distill in 1823. Auchentoshan is the only distillery in Scotland to triple-distill its spirit fully. This method is unusual in Scotland and is more commonly associated with Irish whiskey. The increased copper contact achieved by triple distillation strips impurities from the spirit, and helps to create a lighter style of spirit, resulting in a more easy-drinking style in the finished product.

The distillery was totally rebuilt after World War II, having been severely damaged in a German air raid, and was refurbished in 1984 by Morrison Bowmore (owner of Glen Garioch and Bowmore and now part of Suntory). For many years the only readily available expression was a ten-year-old bottling, which was later supplemented by a release called Three Wood in 2002. The Three Wood release was a favorite of many and was aged in three types of oak casks: ex-bourbon, oloroso sherry, and Pedro Ximénez sherry.

In 2008 the range underwent a complete overhaul and was relaunched with a new design and a handful of new releases, including a 12-year-old expression that replaced the old ten-year-old. The current range features Classic, 12-Year-Old, Three Wood, 18-, and 21-Year-Olds. Five travel retail releases can be also be found under the names Springwood, Heartwood, Cooper's Reserve, Silveroak, and Solera, and there is also a vintage 1974. In 2013 a Virgin Oak cask expression was released in tandem with a Virgin Oak release from Glen Garioch distillery.

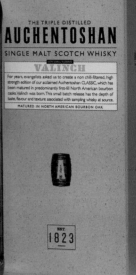

Three Wood

A deep, dark, sherried monster with lashings of rich, macerated fruit flavors, toffee, and milk chocolate.

★ ABV: 43% ★ Type: Single Malt

12-Year-Old

Light and delicate, with a soft, silky mouthfeel and notes of citrus, fruit-and-nut cereal, and caramel.

★ ABV: 64% ★ Type: Single Malt

The lost distilleries

Like all industries, whisky production is subject to the vagaries of economic reality. Rationalization of production has led to the closure of more than 100 distilleries from the high point of the 1800s, when there were more than 200 in Scotland.

However, unlike most industries, whisky has a long afterlife. Even when a distillery closes, a lot of its product remains in warehouses and is increasingly sought after by drinkers eager to taste something that by definition is a finite resource. Not surprisingly, scarcity means that lost-distillery whisky can be highly collectible, with bottles costing hundreds of dollars.

Examples include Brora, formerly the old Clynelish Distillery, which closed in 1983 despite its malt being held in high regard. The whisky is still available from Diageo and independent bottlers, but supplies are running low. The same will eventually be true of whiskies from other lost distilleries, such as Port Ellen, Moffat, Dallas Dhu, and Rosebank.

However, it isn't all doom and gloom. Some distilleries, such as Glen Keith, Glencadam, and Tullibardine, have returned to production as demand for malt continues to grow.

Others are even trying to recreate whiskies of the past. The Lost Distillery Company uses old records of production techniques, machinery, and ingredients to recraft whisky that is as close to the original as possible. It currently has three whiskies: Stratheden, Auchnagie, and Gerston.

Bladnoch

Since Bladnoch was founded in 1817 the distillery has seen many different owners, suffering sporadic production and long periods of being mothballed. The most recent closure came in 1993, when Diageo, or United Distillers as it was known at the time, mothballed Bladnoch, Rosebank, and Pittyvaich distilleries to help manage an overproduction crisis. The following year the distillery was bought by a Northern Irish builder called Raymond Armstrong, although the deal was not without conditions, with United Distillers stipulating that it must not start producing again. In 2000, after determined lobbying by Armstrong and the local community, Diageo finally agreed to revoke the terms of sale and allowed the distillery to resume production, but capped it at 26,500 gallons (100,000 liters) a year. This may sound like a lot, but in Bladnoch's final year of production under United Distillers around 265,000 gallons (one million liters) of spirit were produced.

Nevertheless the distillery was once again working, and in the new millennium spirit flowed again at Bladnoch. The same cannot be said for Rosebank and Pittyvaich, which have both been fully decommissioned. For the first few years the Bladnoch team bottled old stock that had been produced under United. The first release since the reopening came in 2008 in the form of three six-year-old bottlings: a bourbon cask, a sherry cask, and a lightly peated expression. A year later an eight-year-old was released, followed by a number of different releases, both peated and unpeated, from bourbon and sherry casks at ten, 11 and 12 years old. The range from Bladnoch has mainly featured limited and single-cask releases, with the first core expression being released in 2011, called Distiller's Choice.

Distiller's Choice

Sweet floral notes and honeydew melon on the nose, with honey, vanilla, and cereal on the palate leading to canned apricots on the finish.

★ ABV: 46% ★ Type: Single Malt

12-Year-Old Sherry Matured— Sheep Label

Grape, dried fruit, and spice on the nose, with dark, rich fruit on the palate. The finish is intense, fading to summer fruit pudding with vanilla and spice.

★ ABV: 55% ★ Type: Single Malt

Glenkinchie

The Lowland representative in the Classic Malts range, and the closest distillery to Edinburgh, Glenkinchie is arguably the best known of the Lowland malts. Glenkinchie illustrates the Lowland style of whisky perfectly, being light, sweet, and delicate. Glenkinchie and Lowland whisky in general can be a great introductory style for those new to whisky, and ideal for drinking in hotter climes or as an aperitif.

With its close proximity to Edinburgh, Glenkinchie is a pretty major tourist attraction and is well equipped for the tens of thousands of visitors it receives each year, with a museum of distilling occupying the distillery's old malting floor. The distillery can boast some of the largest stills in the industry, with the wash still capable of being charged with 7,925 gallons (30,000 liters) of wash. The stills are so large that the stillhouse roof had to be removed when one of them was replaced in 2008.

Maturation at Glenkinchie takes place mainly in bourbon casks, but the occasional sherry cask is filled in order to make the Distillers Edition, which is aged partly in amontillado sherry casks. Like all whiskies in the Classic Malts selection, Glenkinchie has a small range featuring only two regular bottlings: a 12-year-old and the Distillers Edition.

12-Year-Old

Light, fresh and easygoing, with notes of honey, citrus, heather, vanilla, and sweet fruit.

✴ ABV: 43% ✴ TYPE: Single Malt

Distillers Edition

Richer and with more weight than the 12-Year-Old, with notes of orange zest, spicy stewed fruit, sweet spicy oak, and honey.

✴ ABV: 43% ✴ TYPE: Single Malt

HIGHLANDS

The Wash Act of 1784 determined differential excise levels for Highland and Lowland whiskies, as well as defining which was which. Anything distilled north of the "Highland line" between Greenock and Dundee is considered to be a Highland whisky.

As an exercise in definition, it's fairly blunt. As well as being the largest geographical area, the Highlands is also the hardest region to pin down in terms of style. Highland whiskies can vary massively from light and delicate right through to full bodied and peated. As with all the other regions of Scotland, assigning a

flavor profile to a whisky based on its geographical position is becoming outdated.

In the Northern Highlands the distilleries north of Inverness are all coastal, except Glen Ord, which is only a couple of miles inland. This accounts for a slightly salty taste to Clynelish, Old Pulteney, and Balblair. Also in the north are the light and fragrant Glenmorangie, the sherried Dalmore, and Glen Ord, which is sometimes held to be the best example of the Highland style.

The Southern Highlands produces lighter, fruitier, and drier whiskies such as Edradour—from the

As well as being the largest geographical area, the Highlands is also the hardest region to pin down in terms of style.

smallest distillery in Scotland—and Aberfeldy. The Perthshire distilleries Glenturret, Tulliebardine, Aberfeldy, and Blair Athol lie in the fertile glens of the Tay and its tributaries. To the north is Dalwhinnie, and on the southern edge of the Highlands are Deanston, Glengoyne, and Loch Lomond distilleries.

In the Eastern Highlands full-bodied, dry, fruity malts dominate. Apart from Glen Garioch they have no smokiness. In the north of the region Macduff and Knockdhu touch Speyside, producing whiskies that can be confused with that region. Farther south are Fettercairn and Glencadam, which produces a creamy, fruity malt. Royal Lochnagar and Glendronach sit between the Moray and the Tay.

The Western Highlands has few distilleries still operational, including the coastal Oban and the Ben Nevis Distillery at Fort William.

Ardmore

Founded by Adam Teacher in 1898, the Ardmore distillery has always played an important part in supplying the Teacher's blend, one of the biggest-selling in the United Kingdom. Ardmore stands out from most distilleries on the mainland as it produces a peated whisky, a style normally associated with the Western Isles. In 2007 the first regular distillery bottling for many years was released, called Traditional Cask. This was accompanied by a similar release from Ardmore's sister distillery, Laphroaig on Islay. The whisky has been aged primarily in standard hogshead casks before a final period of maturation in quarter casks. These smaller casks increase the whisky's contact with the wood and accelerate maturation. Aside from the Traditional Cask the range includes 25- and 30-year-olds, the latter being sold only in the United States.

Traditional Cask

A good stepping stone into heavily peated whisky. Smoky bacon potato chips with toffee popcorn and sweet pipe tobacco.

✯ ABV: 46% ✯ Type: Single Malt

Ben Nevis

Sitting at the foot of the U.K.'s highest mountain, the Ben Nevis distillery receives its fair share of visitors but despite this the Ben Nevis whisky isn't hugely well known in the United Kingdom. The distillery has had many twists and turns in its long history, one of the most notable being its 1989 purchase by Nikka, one of the largest players in the Japanese drinks industry. This came about through a historical connection as the founding father of Nikka, Masataka Taketsuru, traveled to Scotland to learn the art of whisky making. The most common bottling is the ten-year-old, but limited releases have occurred along with dozens of independent bottlings.

Ten-Year-Old

A lively whisky with a weighty mouthfeel; notes of chocolate orange, candy apple, and oaky spice dominate.

✯ ABV: 46% ✯ Type: Single Malt

WHAT THEY SAY ...

"Inspiring bold John Barleycorn! What dangers thou canst make us scorn! ... Wi' usquebae, we'll face the devil!"

——Robert Burns

Balblair

The Balblair distillery was first founded in 1790, which places it among the oldest in Scotland. Since its founding the distillery has moved sites up the road and has changed hands a number of times. It was mothballed in 1911 and remained silent until 1949, when production was resumed, but the building was not empty as it was commandeered by the Allied troops during World War II. Unfortunately for the troops stationed there, the distillery was dry.

For the bulk of Balblair's existence the distillery, like many others, has made whisky to be sold to merchants and blenders. Bottlings of Balblair single malt can be found as far back as the 1960s, but it seems these were never released in large quantities. However, in 1996 this was set to change when the distillery was acquired by Inver House Distillers (owners of Pulteney, Knockdhu, and Hankey Bannister, among others), and the malt began to emerge onto the shelves of specialist stores. The new range from Inver House in the 1990s featured a handful of bottlings called Elements, a ten-year-old and a 16-year-old. These were replaced in 2007, when the range was completely overhauled and relaunched in a series of

vintages with a new and distinctive bottle. The new range was hailed a huge success, and the whisky showed what the distillery was really capable of. Production for blends is still a major part of Balblair's business today, with only 10–20 percent of its annual production of 475,000 gallons (1.8 million liters) being bottled and sold as single malt. The latest vintage releases from Balblair include a 2003, 1990, and 1983, but many others can be found, including some very old releases from the 1960s and 1970s.

Balblair 2002

Floral notes and stone fruit on the nose, with lemon toffee and butterscotch on the palate, leading to a light citrusy finish.

✳ ABV: 46% ✳ Type: Single Malt

Balblair 1989

Sweet and spicy on the nose, with citrus, vanilla, and caramel on the palate and fresh fruit and oaky spice on the finish.

✳ ABV: 46% ✳ Type: Single Malt

Blair Athol

Blair Athol is one of only a few distilleries still working today that were operating prior to 1800, making it one of the oldest distilleries in the world. Anyone who drinks whisky in Britain will almost certainly be familiar with Bell's, which was the number one blend in the United Kingdom until usurper Famous Grouse snatched the title in 2006.

Blair Athol plays a major part in Bell's, with the lion's share of the whisky made being used for the blend. Only around five percent is bottled as a single malt and is filled into sherry casks, while the stock destined for blending is filled into ex-bourbon casks. The only regular bottling from the distillery is a 12-year-old in the Flora and Fauna series, but the occasional special release from the distillery has emerged.

12-Year-Old

A mellow whisky at first but over time it evolves into a heavy, fruit-laden, spicy style.

✶ ABV: 43% ✶ Type: Single Malt

The Speaker's choice

It is a tradition in the British House of Commons that the Speaker—the chief officer and highest authority—is allowed to choose his own whisky. The resulting Speaker's Whisky is sold at Westminster and used by the Speaker for entertaining and gifts.

The current Speaker, John Bercow, took up the position in 2009 and opted for a malt bottled by Gordon & MacPhail. The Elgin-based whisky specialist also bottles a House of Commons blended Scotch, and supplies whisky to the Scottish Parliament, the National Assembly for Wales, and the European Parliament.

Although it doesn't state what the whisky is on the bottle, it is believed to be The Macallan. As Bercow is not a whisky connoisseur, he enlisted the aid of Members of Parliament, who conducted a blind taste test. Sales have been relatively brisk, with 1,599 bottles sold in 2011 and 1,662 in 2012.

The previous Speaker, Michael Martin, was also reliant on the aid of his fellow M.P.s in choosing his Speaker's Whisky. The teetotaller took their advice and opted for a ten-year-old The Macallan. When he resigned as Speaker in 2009 the Commons gift shop is reputed to have sold out within hours. It is now sells for almost £200 a bottle.

Betty Boothroyd, the first female Speaker, chose Glendullan 12-year-old for her whisky, Madam Speaker's Order. Her predecessor, Bernard Weatherill, opted for a dram from Caledonian Malt Whisky Distillers.

Clynelish

The Clynelish distillery that stands today was founded in 1967, and was built to replace the old Clynelish distillery across the street during the boom period for whisky that followed World War II. The original Brora distillery had been founded in 1819, and during the whisky downturn of the 1980s a decision had to be made as to which would be closed—the new efficient Clynelish or the aging Brora. The old distillery closed in 1983, but Brora whisky can still be found, and is among the most sought-after whiskies from closed distilleries.

The whisky was once known as the "Islay of the Highlands," and the distillery produced a heavily peated spirit on and off through the 1970s. The new Clynelish was built with the old distillery very much in mind; the new stills for Clynelish were exact replicas of Brora's, and it is said that the Clynelish spirit was much the same. This was just as well, as Brora's spirit had been very popular with blenders, and during the early years of the new Clynelish distillery demand for blended whisky was on the increase.

Clynelish has never had a huge range—a 14-year-old Flora and Fauna bottling could be found in the 1990s which was replaced by a more official release in 2004, also a 14-year-old. The Clynelish range is compact, featuring the aforementioned 14-year-old and a Distillers Edition; recently a 12-year-old was bottled for the "Friends of the Classic Malts" series. Clynelish's popularity with blenders means a number of independent bottlings can be found.

14-Year-Old

Fresh and coastal, with a great range of flavors and quite rich. Notes of honeycomb, citrus, sherbet, and oaky spice appear throughout, along with a subtle earthiness.

✱ ABV: 46% ✱ Type: Single Malt

Distillers Edition

Aged in oloroso seco casks, which lend a rich, fruity character. Sweet sherried fruit flavors bind the coastal character, creating a superb balance between salty and sweet.

✱ ABV: 46% ✱ Type: Single Malt

Dalmore

The Dalmore brand has become one of the most premium malt whiskies in the market and has held the record many times for the most expensive whisky ever sold. The distillery was founded in 1839 by Alexander Matheson, and was built overlooking the Cromarty Firth, an enormous estuary north of Inverness. Its setting is certainly among the most scenic in Scotland. In the years after the distillery was founded it was operated by three brothers, Alexander, Charles, and Andrew Mackenzie, who later bought the distillery after Matheson's death. In 1917 the distillery was commandeered by the Royal Navy, which used the warehousing to assemble mines. When the Navy left, the distillery was in a bad way, having been damaged in a fire caused by an explosion. A long legal battle followed between Andrew Mackenzie and the Navy, as he sought to make it pay for the damage it had caused. In the early 1920s production resumed, and the distillery has operated for many years relatively undisturbed. In 1960 the Mackenzie company merged with Whyte & Mackay, which still has ownership today.

Dalmore produces a whisky that, more often than not, has a large sherry cask influence, but wine, port, and bourbon casks are also used. The range from Dalmore is extensive, and contains some of the most expensive whiskies ever sold, like the Oculus, which contained spirit dating back to 1868 and sold for £27,600 (U.S.$46,000). The range includes 12-, 15-, and 18-year-olds, followed by releases called the Cigar Malt Reserve and King Alexander III. In 2011 the Rivers Collection was launched, from which part of the proceeds goes to the preservation of Scotland's rivers.

15-Year-Old

Rich, fruity, and soft with notes of dried fruit, marzipan, orange marmalade, and rich, oaky spice.

★ ABV: 40% ★ TYPE: Single Malt

Dalmore 18-Year-Old

Soft and silky, with a weighty mouthfeel. The nose is like a box of chocolates and is full and fruity. Notes of candy apple, butterscotch, and spice develop on the palate and finish.

★ ABV: 43% ★ TYPE: Single Malt

Dalwhinnie

Dalwhinnie distillery is located near the Grampian mountain range, on the border of the Cairngorms National Park, and is one of the highest distilleries in Scotland. The distillery is currently under the ownership of Diageo, and since being added to its Classic Malts range in the 1980s has grown in popularity—so much so that it has become one of the best-selling single malts in the Diageo portfolio, along with well-known distilleries such as Talisker and Cardhu.

The distillery was founded in 1897 and got off to a shaky start, changing hands a number of times and being chopped and changed by the various owners. In the 1920s the distillery settled down under the ownership of the Distillers Company Ltd. (DCL) and was licensed to James Buchanan & Co. In 1934, Dalwhinnie was forced to close after a fire and was not reopened until around four years later. The 1980s saw major refurbishment of the distillery, during which a great lesson was learned by the whisky industry. Dalwhinnie had always used worm tubs to condense the spirit vapor of the stills, but during the refurbishment these were removed and replaced by modern and more efficient tube condensers, which are used at most distilleries today.

Once production resumed, it became clear that the new condensers had altered the spirit, and at great cost the worm tubs were reinstalled. A hard lesson learned, but a valuable one. Worm tubs are in use at only a handful of distilleries, four of which sit alongside Dalwhinnie in the Classic Malts range. The Dalwhinnie range features a 15-year-old and the Distillers Edition. A handful of older bottlings have been made available, most recently a 25-year-old Special Release launched in 2012.

15-Year-Old

Soft and easy-drinking with notes of honey, vanilla, sweet spicy fruit, and a subtle trace of peat.

✶ ABV: 43% ✶ TYPE: Single Malt

The Distillers Edition

Sweet, rich fruit on the nose and jammy and thick on the palate, with brown sugar and a toasty, nutty finish.

✶ ABV: 43% ✶ TYPE: Single Malt

Glencadam

Glencadam is sited in the city of Brechin, between Dundee and Aberdeen. The distillery began producing whisky in 1825, only two years after the Excise Act of 1823, which changed the face of the Scottish whisky industry when it legalized distilling. The distillery has seen many different owners over the years, but its current owner is Angus Dundee Distillers (owner of Tomintoul distillery), which acquired the distillery in 2003. The main focus for Angus Dundee is on the sales of blended whisky, but the company has made a good effort to showcase its two distilleries as single malts.

The distillery is capable of producing around 370,000 gallons (1.4 million liters) of spirit a year, most of which is destined for blending. It has one pair of stills which, unlike those of other distilleries, have lyne arms that tilt upward at an angle of 15 degrees. They make it harder for the spirit vapor to run off the still, with any condensing spirit in the lyne arm running back into the still. This means the spirit experiences increased copper contact, which is said to help create sweet, fruity notes in the new-make spirit. Maturation at Glencadam takes place mainly in ex-bourbon casks but some sherry and port casks are filled.

In 2005 Angus Dundee released the first single malt from Glencadam, a 15-year-old bottling that has since been redesigned when the range was relaunched in 2008. The current range features ten-, 15-, and 21-year-olds. These are supplemented by two wood-finished expressions: a 12-year-old Portwood finish and a 14-year-old oloroso cask finish; there are also 30- and 32-year-old single-cask bottlings.

10-Year-Old

Vanilla custard and honey on the nose with citrus and a little bite on the palate, leading to a spicy, slightly peppery finish.

⭐ ABV: 46%
⭐ TYPE: Single Malt

14-Year-Old Oloroso Sherry Cask Finish

Orange peel and chocolate cereal on the nose, with notes of stewed fruit and mixed nuts on the palate and finish.

⭐ ABV: 46%
⭐ TYPE: Single Malt

Glen Garioch

Glen Garioch is part of a small family of distilleries under the ownership of Morison Bowmore, along with Auchentoshan and The Bowmore. In the mid-1990s, Morrison Bowmore was acquired by giant Japanese drinks company Suntory. This gave Suntory its first footings in the Scotch whisky industry, and since then those distilleries have prospered. Glen Garioch is among Scotland's oldest distilleries, founded in 1797 in Old Meldrum in the eastern Highlands, not far from Aberdeen. With a rich history of whisky making for over 200 years, the distillery is no stranger to progress, creating a hugely innovative waste heat recovery system in the 1970s, called the Greenhouse Project, which generated a lot of media attention at the time.

The distillery is enjoying a revival of late, and since a full relaunch of its range in 2009 has been receiving high praise from enthusiasts. The decision was taken with the new range to bottle at a higher ABV of 48 percent and with no chill-filtration: two surefire ways to get enthusiasts on board. At the heart of the range is the Founder's Reserve, followed by a 12-year-old, both of which are aged in a combination of ex-bourbon and ex-sherry casks. These are supplemented with a series of vintage releases, all bottled at cask strength, which over the last few years have included 1999, 1997, 1995, 1994, 1991, 1990, 1986, and a 1978. Alongside these, a number of travel retail bottlings have been released. Most recently came a Virgin Oak expression released in tandem with a Virgin Oak-matured Auchentoshan. Both peated and unpeated spirit has been made at Glen Garioch over the years, with some older releases displaying noticeable peaty characteristics not found in newer, younger bottlings.

12-Year-Old

A powerful whisky with plenty of character and a deep, dark, fruity, nutty, chocolaty flavor.

⋆ ABV: 48% ⋆ Type: Single Malt

1995

Banana caramel pie and mocha on the nose; dried fruit, hazelnut, subtle smoke, and chocolate granola on the palate and finish.

⋆ ABV: 55.3% ⋆ Type: Single Malt

Glengoyne

The Glengoyne distillery is located in the southern Highlands, just outside Glasgow, and began making whisky in 1833. The distillery has seen a number of different owners in its lifetime, but currently it is in the hands of Ian MacLeod Distillers, which bought it in 2003. Previously it was under the ownership of Edrington. In the last ten years the distillery and the Glengoyne range have gone from strength to strength.

The malted barley used at Glengoyne is dried with warm air and without any peat influence. With a totally unpeated spirit the whisky appeals to a wide audience and is very approachable. Glengoyne practices an incredibly slow distillation, which it describes as "nursing the spirit through the stills," prolonging copper contact to create a sweeter taste. It also operates three stills, which is an oddity, as stills usually work in pairs: a wash still and a spirit still. However, at Glengoyne they have two spirit stills running in tandem. Glengoyne, like Glenfarclas, The GlenDronach, and Highland Park, is a strong advocate of the sherry cask, and invests huge sums sourcing these casks from Spain.

From the point where the Spanish oak tree is felled to make a cask it takes roughly four years before it will be filled at Glengoyne. The oak is air dried naturally, and after being coopered into a sherry butt (500-liter/133-gallon cask) it is then seasoned with oloroso sherry for nearly two years before being emptied and sent to Scotland. The range from Glengoyne was recently revised and includes 10-, 12-, 15-, 18-, and 21-year-olds. As well as these a duty free range can be found. Recently discontinued bottlings include the 17- and 12-year-old cask strength.

Cask Strength

A subtle nose with hints of dried fruit. The palate is full and weighty with hard candy and spice leading to cotton candy, ginger, and fruitcake on the finish.

✶ ABV: 58.7% ✶ TYPE: Single Malt

15-Year-Old

Soft and fruity on the nose, with vanilla, honey, and Frosted Flakes cereal on the palate leading to a soft, fruity, spicy finish.

✶ ABV: 43% ✶ TYPE: Single Malt

Glenmorangie

Glenmorangie is one of the best-selling malt whiskies in the world and is available in most liquor stores, meaning you usually don't have to go too far to find a bottle. The distillery was founded in 1843 and is located near Tain, in the northern Highlands. The distillery was established by William Matheson, who started it with a pair of secondhand gin stills. These tall stills have become an intrinsic part of the Glenmorangie spirit style and are currently the tallest stills in the industry, standing at 18 feet tall—roughly the same height as an adult giraffe. The length of the neck on the still means the spirit has to work hard to reach the top and make it over the lyne arm to the condenser. This results in increased copper contact and a lighter, fruitier spirit style. The original gin stills have long since been replaced, but replicas have been made, and after an expansion in 1990 now total eight.

In order to make good whisky you need good casks, and few understand this better than Glenmorangie. Over the years the company has made a huge effort to create some of the best casks in use in the whisky industry. This obsession with creating the best casks led Glenmorangie to the oak forests of the Ozark Mountains in Missouri, U.S.A. Slow-growth American white oak trees are selected, felled, milled, and left to air dry naturally before being coopered and charred with great precision. These casks are then lent to an undisclosed whiskey producer in Kentucky and another producer in Tennessee, where they are seasoned for four years with either bourbon or Tennessee whiskey, after which they are shipped to Glenmorangie to be filled. Glenmorangie also uses a number of other casks in maturation, including port, Sauternes, sherry, and wine casks, all of which are scrutinized by the whisky creation team before being gathered and filled at the distillery.

Various European casks are used to create the wood-finished expressions in the Glenmorangie range. These are whiskies where the spirit has been aged primarily in American oak, and then transferred to any of the aforementioned casks for a final period of maturation. This technique was spearheaded by Glenmorangie in the 1990s, although there is some debate about where the idea originated. The Glenmorangie range features a huge number of whiskies, including the Original (ten-year-old), Quinta Ruban (port cask finish), Nectar D'Or (Sauternes finish), and Lasanta (sherry finish).

Original

Light and delicate with sweet toffee, vanilla, and citrus flavors. Perfect for recruiting whisky drinkers.

✦ ABV: 40% ✦ TYPE: Single Malt

Quinta Ruban
12-Year-Old

Chocolate orange on the nose with sweet, jammy fruit, dark chocolate, and spice on the palate and finish.

✦ ABV: 46% ✦ TYPE: Single Malt

Signet

Made using a proportion of chocolate malt, normally used for stouts and porters. Rich, deep, dark, and complex with dark fruit, mocha, vanilla, and oaky spice.

✦ ABV: 46% ✦ TYPE: Single Malt

Glen Moray

In 2008 Glen Moray underwent a tectonic shift in ownership, as it was bought by French spirits company La Martiniquaise. Prior to this Glen Moray had been under the ownership of Glenmorangie PLC, and although it enjoyed many years of steady growth it had always played the underdog to the company's other two distilleries, Glenmorangie and Ardbeg. Since the takeover a handful of new releases have emerged, and the distillery is beginning to grow out of the shadow of Glenmorangie. The current range includes Classic and 10-, 12-, and 16-year-olds, while a handful of older expressions are also available, including a 25- and a 30-year-old. Independent bottlings can be found but have become less frequent since the change in ownership.

12-Year-Old

An easygoing style with notes of freshly sliced pear, vanilla, rhubarb and custard candies, and shortbread.

✴ ABV: 40% ✴ TYPE: Single Malt

Knockdhu

It's rare for a distillery to sell its malt whisky under a different name, but Knockdhu does just that. The owner first made the decision in 1993 to release the whisky under the name AnCnoc in order to differentiate its whisky from the Knockando distillery. After a few teething problems and switching between the two names in 2003 they finally settled on the name AnCnoc. Together with the new(ish) name, a new contemporary design and a top-notch whisky, the brand soon gained traction with whisky fans. The range includes 12-, 16-, and 22-year-olds, and these are supplemented each year with a vintage bottling. In 2012 a limited edition 35-year-old was released, as well as an unusual series with labels designed by illustrator Peter Arkle.

AnCnoc 12-Year-Old

A subtle and complex whisky with a range of flavors developing throughout. Stewed, spicy fruits combine with subtle smoke.

✴ ABV: 40% ✴ TYPE: Single Malt

WHAT THEY SAY ...

"They say some of my stars drink whiskey, but I have found that ones who drink milkshakes don't win many ball games."

—Casey Stenge

Oban

Oban is one of only ten distilleries working today that were built before 1800. Throughout the last two centuries it has weathered many storms and climbed steadily into the top 20 best-selling single malts worldwide. Part of this success is due to its placement in Diageo's Classic Malts range in 1988. As well as being one of the oldest distilleries, Oban is one of the smallest, and because of its remote location on the west coast, in the center of a small fishing town where there are other buildings in close proximity, any expansion is impossible. Oban has a tiny range consisting of only two expressions, namely the classic 14-year-old and The Distillers Edition. The latter is released each year and is finished in Montilla fino sherry casks. Independent bottlings are nearly impossible to find.

14-Year-Old

Perfect for those who like a coastal style but are not fans of heavy peat. This whisky is a great all-rounder, fruity and soft, but also spicy and slightly smoky.

★ ABV: 43% ★ TYPE: Single Malt

Old Pulteney

The Pulteney distillery is the second most northerly distillery on the mainland and can be found in the old fishing town of Wick. The distillery was founded in 1826 by James Henderson, in what was at the time one of the busiest fishing ports in Europe. It's said that in its heyday the port attracted around 1,000 fishing vessels with around 7,000 workers, all making a living from the "silver darlings" otherwise known as herring. The distillery has changed hands a number of times since it was founded, seeing at least half a dozen different owners. It was in 1997 that current owner Inver House Distillers (owners of Balblair, Knockdhu, and Speyburn distilleries) acquired the distillery. It was also the same year that the staple whisky from the distillery was launched, the Old Pulteney 12-Year-Old.

Pulteney is very much a coastal distillery, and is just a stone's throw from the coastline. This coastal connection runs deep in the whisky, and some believe that the sea air imbues the maturing spirit with a fresh character and subtle dry saltiness—a theory not completely without merit, as oak is porous and casks do breathe. The distillery also sponsors a number of seaworthy events, most recently backing a yacht that was entered into the Clipper 2013–14 Round the World Yacht Race. Since Inver House took over, Pulteney sales have been on the up, with many of its whiskies scooping medals in various competitions. The range includes 12-, 17-, 21-, 30-, and 40-year-olds, and these are supplemented with a handful of limited and travel retail releases.

17-Year-Old

Light and sweet on the nose with stewed pears and candy apple on the palate and traces of vanilla on the finish.

★ ABV: 46% ★ TYPE: Single Malt

12-Year-Old

Fresh, feisty, and undoubtedly coastal. Notes of citrus, honey, pine, malt, and oak appearing throughout.

★ ABV: 40% ★ TYPE: Single Malt

Royal Lochnagar

Lochnagar and its founder, James Robertson, didn't have the best of luck when starting out. After his first distillery at Glen Feardan was burned to the ground in 1826 by competitors, James built Lochnagar. It wasn't long before this distillery shared the same fate, giving reason to believe that James was not a popular fellow. In 1845 the distillery that stands today was built and aptly named New Lochnagar. By now the Victorian era was in full swing and during a passing visit in 1848 Queen Victoria issued the distillery with a royal warrant, adding the "Royal" to Royal Lochnagar. It is the smallest distillery in the Diageo family, and a small range of a 12-year-old, Distillers Edition, and Select Reserve are the only core bottlings.

12-Year-Old

A complex whisky with a huge range of flavors, notes of toffee, dried fruit, oaky spice, licorice, and a very subtle herbaceous note.

✵ ABV: 43% ✵ Type: Single Malt

A singular experience

Even the most exclusive malts are combinations of whisky from different barrels and different years, as a distillery will seek to maintain the consistency of its whisky over time.

However, every barrel of whisky is subtly different, influenced by the type of cask used, its position in the warehouse, and even the weather. Single-cask whisky allows a drinker to experience the unique taste of an individual barrel that has not been mixed or even chill-filtered.

Because every barrel is unique, it may yield only a couple hundred bottles. Each bottle usually bears the barrel number, the date of aging, and the number of bottles produced. They tend to sell at a premium compared to standard whisky and can be highly collectible.

Single-cask whisky is typically at cask strength of 50–60 percent ABV, as opposed to the more standard 40–43 percent. It is usually drunk with spring water, to individual taste.

Although connoisseurs maintain that single cask is whisky as it should be, knowing the provenance of the whisky is no guarantee that it will taste great. Blending works because it helps enhance the qualities of a whisky and compensates for weaknesses.

That said, there are plenty of takers for single-cask whisky. Some distilleries, such as Glengoyne, let you choose the barrel, attend tastings, and even bring your cask a birthday cake!

Tomatin

During the 1970s Tomatin operated an incredible 23 stills, making it, if only for a short time, the largest distillery in Scotland. During these glory years the distillery was capable of producing around 3.2 million gallons (12 million liters) a year. That's equivalent to some of Scotland's megadistilleries built recently to cater for the latest whisky boom. During the early 1980s, however, Tomatin went through troubled times and its capacity was greatly reduced. In 1986 Tomatin became the first Scottish distillery to be owned by the Japanese, and through this acquisition it was saved. The range includes Legacy, 12-, 15-, 18-, and 30-year-olds, a peated release called Cù Bòcan, and a handful of limited expressions.

12-Year-Old

A very easygoing and straightforward malt. Notes of caramel, vanilla, citrus, and candy apple work together to form an enjoyable dram.

✶ ABV: 40% ✶ TYPE: Single Malt

Tullibardine

After nearly ten years of being mothballed under the ownership of Whyte & Mackay, new life was breathed into Tullibardine in 2003, when it was bought by a group of private investors. The new owners set about releasing a plethora of new releases, while fully embracing the idea of finishing in various casks. In 2011 the distillery changed hands again and was bought by a French company called Picard Vins & Spiritueux. The new owner has kept things at the distillery much the same, and has set about tidying up the range, releasing some core expressions, namely Sovereign (NAS), three wood-finished expressions called 225 Sauternes, 228 Burgundy, and 500 Sherry, and 20- and 25-year-olds.

Sovereign

This whisky is aged entirely in ex-bourbon casks and is very approachable. A subtle combination of vanilla and caramel ties in with floral notes to create a light, delicate dram.

✶ ABV: 43% ✶ TYPE: Single Malt

ISLAY

This small island off the west coast of Scotland is sometimes called "Whisky Island" owing to its concentration of distilleries. There are eight working distilleries within its 240 square miles, and a ninth, Gartbeck, is planned.

As the historic base of the regional kings known as the "Lords of the Isles," Islay has a history of independence, which is echoed in the unique flavors of its malt whisky. The island's topography has helped create some of the strongest-flavored malt whiskies. Islay has large areas of peat bog, so it is unsurprising that its malts are often high in phenols. Winter gales drive salt spray inland to saturate the peat, adding

The island's topography has helped create some of the strongest-flavored malt whiskies.

another distinction to Islay whisky. When used to dry the barley for Lagavulin, Ardbeg, and Laphroaig, the result is a powerful, almost medicinal taste, saturated with peat smoke, brine, and iodine.

To the north of the island, the distilleries produce a quite different whisky. Bruichladdich, which reopened in 2001, and Bunnahabhain draw spring water before

it has had contact with peat. They also use lightly peated or unpeated barley, so their house style whiskies are milder and lighter as a result. To confuse things, however, Bruichladdich also produces what it claims is the most heavily peated whisky in the world: Octomore.

The Bowmore distillery, in the middle of the island, has a taste somewhere between the northern and southern Islay whiskies. It has some peat but is not medicinal, with toffee and floral traces. Caol Ila is a briny, smoky whisky from Islay's biggest distillery. It is a relative newcomer as a single malt, and is a prominent malt used in many blends.

Finally, the island's newest distillery, Kilchoman, opened in 2005 and takes the Islay spirit of independence to the extreme, with all stages of production taking place on the island, including growing its own barley.

Ardbeg

The Ardbeg distillery sits on the south coast of Islay along with Lagavulin and Laphroaig. Like its neighboring distilleries, Ardbeg makes a heavily peated style of whisky. The distillery was founded in 1815, although distilling had been taking place on the site as early as 1794, and operated successfully for nearly two centuries until 1981, when it closed. Thankfully this was not the end of Ardbeg, as the distillery was bought by the Glenmorangie Company in 1997. This marked a new chapter and the beginnings of what would become one of the most iconic Islay malt whiskies. With Glenmorangie at the helm production was resumed, and a string of bottlings using the previous stocks were released.

These nineties releases included some incredible expressions that can now reach dizzying prices at auction and are highly prized by Ardbeg fans.

In 2004 the first new Ardbeg, using spirit distilled since the reopening, was launched, and called Very Young. This was the first in a series that would follow until the whisky reached ten years old, the age of the main distillery bottling. Still Young and Almost There releases followed, and in 2008 Renaissance was released, marking the ten years since reopening. Like most distilleries on Islay, Ardbeg buys in its malt from Port Ellen maltings, and fills its spirit into ex-bourbon casks. In Ardbeg's case casks from Buffalo Trace Distillery account for the majority of fills, but some sherry and other casks are also filled. The current range includes a 10-year-old, Uigeadail, and Corryvreckan. Each year a limited expression is released, and recently these have included Ardbog, Galileo, and Alligator. Numerous single-cask bottlings emerged after the reopening.

10-Year-Old

Intense smoke on the nose, with sweet citrus, honey, peat, and more smoke on the palate and finish.

✴ ABV: 46%
✴ Type: Single Malt

Uigeadail

Matured partially in sherry casks. Smoky chocolate on the nose with fruitcake and peat on the palate, leading to a long, firm finish with plenty of grip.

✴ ABV: 54.2%
✴ Type: Single Malt

Bowmore

The Bowmore distillery lies in the heart of the island in the village of Bowmore, Islay's "capital." The distillery is the oldest on Islay, and also among the oldest in Scotland, having been founded in 1779 by John Simpson. In the years that followed, the distillery saw many different owners, but in 1963 Stanley P. Morrison bought it for the princely sum of £117,000 (U.S.$333,000), and formed the company Morrison Bowmore (owner of Glen Garioch and Auchentoshan). The company grew and was bought by its current owner, Suntory, in 1994.

Bowmore is one of only a handful of distilleries in Scotland that still has a working malting floor, producing around one third of the distillery's malt, the rest being brought in from Port Ellen maltings. Unlike Islay's heavyweights Ardbeg, Lagavulin, and Laphroaig, Bowmore's whisky is not as heavily peated, with its malt peated to roughly half the amount of the others. The distillery claims to be one of the best on the island, with a view over the large sea bay, Loch Indal, and a very slick, modern visitor center. Bowmore matures its spirit in a number of different cask types, including ex-bourbon and sherry, and has been known to fill wine and port casks, although not regularly.

The range from Bowmore is enormous, and contains some incredibly expensive and old releases, including Bowmore White, Gold, and Black, which were released between 2007–09 and sell for thousands. The current range features Legend, 12 Years Old, 15 Years Old "Darkest" (sherry cask), 18-, and 25-year-olds. Travel retail releases include Surf, 12 Years Old Enigma, 15 Years Old Mariner, 17 Years Old, and 100 degrees proof. Recent limited releases have included the Tempest series and the Devil's Casks, a 23-year-old aged in port casks.

Tempest 10 Years Old, Batch 4

Aged in first-fill bourbon casks. Notes of citrus, vanilla soft smoke, peat, pepper, and oaky spice.

✻ ABV: 55.1% ✻ Type: Single Malt

15-Year-Old Darkest

Smoke, fruit, and antiseptic cream on the nose, with toffee and spicy fruit on the palate, leading to smoky, dry finish.

✻ ABV: 43% ✻ Type: Single Malt

Bruichladdich

The Bruichladdich distillery lies on the west of the island, near the village of Port Charlotte. It was founded in 1881 by the Harvey brothers, William, John, and Robert, who between them managed to build what was at the time a state-of-the-art Victorian distillery. The Harveys had deep roots in whisky production, owning and operating a number of distilleries on the mainland. Their new distillery enjoyed many years of success until the death of William in 1937, when it closed. The following year it reopened, but the next few decades for Bruichladdich were set to be turbulent, with many different owners and spells of closure.

The turning point came in 2000, when the distillery was bought by a private investor group that included local landowners. With the distillery now under independent ownership, a new spirit of authenticity and pride emerged. Today, the distillery employs nearly 50 local people, one of whom is three times Distiller of the Year Jim McEwan, who joined as head of production after many years working at Bowmore.

Bruichladdich has many unique qualities, not least that the distillery is a working time machine with nearly all its original equipment having been restored. It operates one of only two Lomond stills in existence

(albeit to make gin; the other is at Scapa). Every cask filled is matured on Islay, and all barley used for production, a percentage of which is organic, is grown in Scotland. Since 2000 the distillery has been a runaway success, so much so that in 2012 it caught the eye of large spirits company Rémy Cointreau, which managed to buy it for the sum of £58 million (U.S.$97 million): not a bad return for the investors who bought it for £6.5 million ($9.8 million).

The distillery makes three different types of whisky: unpeated, sold under the name Bruichladdich; heavily peated, sold under the name Port Charlotte; and super-heavily peated, sold under the name Octomore. Octomore is currently the most heavily peated whisky in the world. Maturation takes place in many cask types, including ex-bourbon, and dozens of different wine casks. Among the three different styles there have been more releases than any other distillery. Some of the latest and consistent releases include the Laddie Ten, the Laddie 16 and the Laddie 22, Bere Barley 2006 2nd edition, Islay Barley 2007—Rockside Farm, Black Arts 3 and 4, Port Charlotte 10, Octomore 10, Octomore 06.1, and Octomore 06.2. Bruichladdich adds no coloring and never chill-filters.

The Laddie Ten

Slightly sweet, with green notes on the nose. Sweet and light on the palate with a dry, salty, earthy finish.

★ ABV: 46% ★ Type: Single Malt

Port Charlotte Ten-Year-Old

Smoke, citrus, and heather on the nose with ripe fruit and peat on the palate and a spicy, smoky finish.

★ ABV: 46% ★ Type: Single Malt

Octomore 06.1

A complex and intense whisky but with a light mouthfeel. Plenty of peat, ash, honey, citrus, and sea spray. The finish is peppery, dry, salty, smoky, and intense.

★ ABV: 57% ★ Type: Single Malt

Bunnahabhain

Bunnahabhain is the most northerly distillery on the island, and unlike the other distilleries is not famous for making a peated style of whisky. Instead, the house style whisky from Bunnahabhain is much lighter than its neighbors. However, the distillery does make peated whisky and plenty of it, the vast majority of which is sold to blenders and bottlers; interestingly this spirit goes by the name Margadale, after a local river. Margadale is becoming increasingly popular among the independent bottlers, as not only does it taste excellent, but the other distilleries on Islay are willing to sell fewer casks to independent bottlers and blenders. This is mainly because of the rising demand for peated whisky, meaning that distilleries like Laphroaig, Lagavulin, and Ardbeg need every drop for their single malts, selling very few casks to independents, if any.

In the same way, Islay's giant distillery, Caol Ila, needs all the casks it can fill to meet the global demand for Johnnie Walker, in which it plays an intrinsic role. This means in the coming years we could see a lot more peated whisky coming out of Bunnahabhain, but this is unlikely ever to affect the house style. A peated whisky does appear in the Bunnahabhain range as a ten-year-old under the name Toiteach (pronounced *toch-chach*), but it is not yet as widely available as the rest of the range. The distillery is currently under the ownership of Burn Stewart Distillers (owners of Tobermory and Deanston) and can produce around 715,000 gallons (2.7 million liters) of spirit. The range includes 12-, 18-, and 25-year-olds. Older releases and independent bottlings can also be found.

12-Year-Old

Fresh and light on the nose with traces of fruit on the palate and subtle, soft peat on the finish.

✦ ABV: 46.3% ✦ TYPE: Single Malt

18-Year-Old

Rich and sweet on the nose, with a big fruity, sherry presence on the palate and a dry, salty finish..

✦ ABV: 46.3% ✦ TYPE: Single Malt

Caol Ila

The Caol Ila Distillery was founded in 1846 and sits overlooking the narrow gap of sea called the Sound of Islay, from which the distillery takes its name. The view from the stillhouse is one of the most scenic of any distillery, with the sea and the Paps of Jura framed in the huge windows. Caol Ila is the largest distillery on Islay, and after expansion in 2011 is now capable of producing a staggering 1.7 million gallons (6.5 million liters) of spirit a year, almost twice as much as the second largest on the island, Laphroaig.

The vast majority of whisky produced by Caol Ila is destined to be blended on the mainland. Caol Ila plays an important role in many of the world's most popular blends, but mostly the famous Johnnie Walker. Aside from playing a key role in Diageo's blending program, the distillery produces a popular single malt in its own right, which has become more widely available in recent years. The current range from the distillery includes Moch, 12-, 18-, and 25-year-olds, the Distillers Edition (finished in Moscatel wine casks), and Cask Strength. Caol Ila ages almost entirely in American oak casks, but the occasional sherry cask release can be found, like the Managers' Choice release in 2010. An unpeated release and a number of independent bottlings from various companies can be found, some of which can be great value for money.

12-Year-Old

Soft peat smoke meets a sea breeze on the nose with citrus, spice, and a distinctive coastal character on the palate. A more delicate dram compared to some of its neighbors.

★ ABV: 43% ★ TYPE: Single Malt

Distillers Edition

Spicy, rich fruit and smoke on the nose with peat, honey, and smoke on the palate and a sweet, spicy finish.

★ ABV: 43% ★ TYPE: Single Malt

WHAT THEY SAY . . .

"A good gulp of hot whisky at bedtime—it's not very scientific, but it helps."

—Sir Alexander Fleming

Kilchoman

Kilchoman is Islay's newest distillery, and on its completion in 2005 was the first distillery to be built in Islay in over a hundred years. The distillery was set up by Antony Wills, who is the company director, but it is managed by John MacLellan, former manager at Bunnahabhain. The distillery is tiny compared to its neighbors and lies on the west of the island, not far from Bruichladdich, within the grounds of Rockside Farm, which supplies some of the malt used in production.

Kilchoman operates its own malting floor and takes care of all its own bottling. Every cask filled is matured on Islay, and work is currently under way to expand the warehousing to provide a home for future casks. Kilchoman has already outgrown its own warehousing and is having to store a number of casks in the buildings of the closed Port Ellen distillery.

The distillery is currently going from strength to strength and has done an amazing job in championing the merits of young whisky. In 2009 the first Kilchoman single malt was released at three years old, followed by three new releases in 2010. In 2011 Kilchoman released the first whisky in a series called 100% Islay. These releases use only Islay-grown malt that has been malted at the distillery and, compared with the standard releases, are less heavily peated. This series is currently on its third release. The range from Kilchoman has mainly focused on limited releases, but two core expressions can be found, called Machir Bay and Loch Gorm (Sherry Cask). Kilchoman adds no coloring and doesn't chill-filter.

100% Islay 3rd edition

Light with sweet smoke on the nose and notes of citrusy toffee, gentle peat, butterscotch, crisp barley, and smoke.

★ ABV: 50% ★ Type: Single Malt

Machir Bay

Bold smoke and citrus on the nose, with candy apple and peat on the palate, oaky spice and smoke on the finish.

★ ABV: 46% ★ Type: Single Malt

Small is beautiful

In the nineteenth century farm distilleries were common on Islay, as the Small Stills Act of 1816 encouraged distillers to take out licenses for stills with a maximum capacity of 40 gallons. Few survived the economics of the age, but fast-forward almost two centuries and the spirit of farmscale distilling was reawakened by Anthony Wills, founder and owner of Kilchoman. A former independent bottler, he raised £1 million (U.S.$1.8 million) to launch an artisan whisky operation at Rockside Farm in the parish of Kilchoman on Islay. Its two stills only hold around 793 gallons (3,000 liters) between them and volume-wise could fit several times over in the stills of its neighboring distilleries.

Production is around 31,700 gallons (120,000 liters) a year and began in 2005 with a peaty spirit that would mature quickly. Kilchoman's first single malt was released as a three-year-old in September 2009.

A unique aspect of Kilchoman is that it produces whisky from field to glass, growing and malting barley, distilling spirit and maturing it on the farm. The result is Inaugural 100% Islay Edition, a limited bottling first released in June 2011.

The idea of taking whisky back to its roots has struck a chord with enthusiasts. Kilchoman was named the Whisky of the Year in the 2013 International Whisky Competition, beating 50 other drams in a blind taste test.

Lagavulin

In 1816 John Johnston, an Islay farmer and most likely an illicit distiller, founded the Lagavulin distillery on the south coast of the island. It is located in view of the historic Dunyvaig Castle, which was, many centuries ago, the naval stronghold of the Lords of the Isles. In 1852 the distillery changed hands and was acquired by Alexander Graham, who ran the site until 1867. At this point James Logan Mackie & Co. stepped in and set about refurbishing the distillery and streamlining production.

It was during this period of ownership that the distillery really began to take off. Around 1878 it also saw one of its most notable figures, Peter Mackie, come on board. Peter eventually ended up inheriting the distillery and creating the White Horse blend, which is still popular today. He was also the instigator of the Malt Mill distillery, which was built within the site in 1908 and closed in 1960. The elusive and infamous Malt Mill whisky is the holy grail of Islay whisky, with only one bottle known to be in existence, which is kept in the visitor center at the distillery.

Few distilleries share the kind of success that Lagavulin has experienced over the last 20–30 years, with the Lagavulin 16-Year-Old among the most famous malt whiskies in the world. This success means that the distillery is currently working nonstop to ensure there is enough stock for the future. Because of its popularity Lagavulin keeps all it produces, except for a small amount rumored to be set aside for the White Horse blend. The Lagavulin range features a 16-year-old, The Distillers Edition, and a Cask Strength 12-year-old. A handful of other releases have been made available, most recently a 37-year-old special release from 2013.

16-Year-Old

Intense peat and smoke on the nose with a weighty mouthfeel. Notes of seaweed, sweet peat, smoky bacon potato chips and dried fruit.

✶ ABV: 43% ✶ TYPE: Single Malt

The Distillers Edition

Smoky dried fruit on the nose, with sweet ripe fruit and peat on the palate with a dry, salty, savory finish.

✶ ABV: 43% ✶ TYPE: Single Malt

Laphroaig

The Laphroaig distillery sits on the south coast of Islay next door to Lagavulin, and produces Islay's best-selling single malt. Laphroaig also features in the top ten malt whiskies sold worldwide. Laphroaig is one of only a handful of distilleries left in Scotland that still have a working malting floor; it supplies around a fifth of the distillery's malt, the rest being brought in from the Port Ellen maltings. The distillery operates seven stills in total and is capable of producing around 872,000 gallons (3.3 million liters) of spirit a year. Maturation takes place in ex-bourbon casks, which are sourced from the Maker's Mark distillery in Kentucky. The two distilleries are linked, as both are owned by Beam.

Laphroaig is undoubtedly a big, peaty whisky with a taste that many perceive as medicinal, like iodine or antiseptic. These flavor traits were of major benefit to it in the 1920s, when Prohibition was under way in the United States. Laphroaig somehow managed to escape the ban, being sold for medicinal purposes. Laphroaig has one of the largest distillery-led whisky societies in the "Friends of Laphroaig," which has over half a million members worldwide. By joining you're entitled to a free dram when visiting the distillery, and a discount in the shop. You also receive your very own square foot of Islay in a field across the road from the distillery, which you can mark with a flag. The current range from Laphroaig includes Quarter Cask, 10-Year-Old, 10-Year-Old cask strength, Triple Wood, and 18- and 25-year-olds. Travel retail features PX Cask (aged in Pedro Ximénez casks), QA Cask, and An Cuan Mor. A collection of older bottlings and a Cairdeas series can also be found.

Quarter Cask

The smaller casks intensify the maturation process. Caramel and vanilla mingle with sweet peat and smoke.

★ ABV: 48% ★ Type: Single Malt

18-Year-Old

Less intense than the Quarter Cask with a big, rich mouthfeel and notes of toffee, dried fruit and nuts, seaweed, and smoke.

★ ABV: 48% ★ Type: Single Malt

THE ISLANDS

Strictly speaking, the Scottish islands are not a whisky region in their own right but are considered part of the Highlands region. However, the term is commonly used to describe the sparse scattering of whiskies produced in the islands around the Scottish mainland.

As with other parts of Scotland, there were once many more distilleries here. The Isle of Arran alone had about 50 legal and illegal distillers 200 years ago. Most farmers used leftover barley to make whisky. Over time the number has declined dramatically, so that there are now only seven distillers in all the Scottish islands; however, the whiskies are extremely diverse.

Arran's current distillery dates from 1995. Its delicate whiskies have recently come of age and are described as malty, rich, and fruity, with no peat. However, there are some peated trials.

On Jura, proximity to the sea leads to a slightly salty, smoky flavor in the oily and gently peated whisky of its one distillery. The Isle of Skye's distillery, Talisker, creator of "The Lava of the Cuillins," uses a peated malt, and the smoky, pungent whisky is similar in style to the peat monsters from Islay's southern coast.

Mull also has a solitary distillery, which produces Tobermory, a sweet, thick, slightly herbal whisky, and a heavily peated version called Ledaig.

Mull also has a solitary distillery, which produces Tobermory, a sweet, thick, slightly herbal whisky.

To the north, Orkney's single malts from Highland Park are coastal and full, with plenty of honey, heather, and smoky malt. The other Orcadian distillery, Scapa, produces whisky with a citrus and herbal quality.

New whiskies are cropping up in the islands. The Abhainn Dearg, or Red River, distillery on the west coast of Lewis claims to be the most westerly in Scotland. It opened in 2008 and released its first spirit in 2010. On Barra in the Orkneys, plans are afoot for a niche microdistillery that will grow its own barley and generate power through wind turbines.

Arran

The Arran distillery is the only one on the island of Arran, and sits on the north of the island, just outside the picturesque village of Lochranza. Despite its remote location it receives around 60,000 visitors a year. The distillery was founded in 1993, the same year that Diageo closed the Rosebank, Pittyvaich, and Bladnoch distilleries. Setting up a distillery at this time was no doubt seen as madness, but with the coming of the recent whisky boom, it has turned out to be a prudent move. The distillery started producing in 1995, and by 1998 had its first single malt on the market.

The following years saw many different young expressions emerge, including a handful of vintage bottlings and around a dozen different cask finishes. These included Calvados, Cognac, Marsala, port, and a selection of pretty flashy wine casks such as Château Margaux and *grand cru* Champagne. In 2006 Arran launched its ten-year-old whisky, which was greeted with open arms by those who had been following the distillery's progress through its early releases. The distillery continued to release new expressions and soon gained traction on the malt whisky scene, with some of its releases being highly praised. In 2008 the Arran 12-Year-Old was released, followed by a couple of peated single cask releases and some more wood finishes in 2009. The year 2010 saw the arrival of a 14-year-old and the peated Machrie Moor release, as well as an interesting release called Rowan Tree. In 2012 the Eagle was launched, most likely taking its name from the two golden eagles nesting near the distillery, and the Devil's Punch Bowl. In 2013 Arran produced the oldest bottling to date, a 16-year-old. Unlike many island malts Arran's house style is unpeated.

10-Year-Old

A light, fresh, and easygoing whisky and a great alternative to a lot of Speysiders. Notes of vanilla, toffee, and citrus appear throughout.

✴ ABV: 46% ✴ Type: Single Malt

14-Year-Old

Lush and fruity on the nose with vanilla, lemon cake, and dried fruit on the palate, with a spicy, nutty finish.

✴ ABV: 46% ✴ Type: Single Malt

Scapa

The Orkney Isles are home to two distilleries, Highland Park and Scapa. Of the two, it is fair to say that Scapa is the lesser known, no doubt because it was built around a hundred years later, in 1885, and for long periods of time only operated for a few months each year. In 2004 the distillery underwent a huge £2.1 million (U.S.$3.8 million) refurbishment, essentially saving it from permanent closure. Scapa has some unusual quirks; it exclusively fills American oak casks and makes a completely unpeated spirit, almost the complete opposite to its neighbor. It also operates an unusual type of still called a Lomond still, of which only two survive in Scotland today. The lack of mature stock means that only one official bottling is available, a 16-year-old expression, which replaced the 14-year-old in 2008.

16-Year-Old

Fresh fruity flavors intertwine with oaky spice and vanilla custard. An assertive whisky with a weighty mouthfeel and bags of character.

★ ABV: 40% ★ TYPE: Single Malt

Highland Park

Highland Park distillery is located in the Orkney Isles and is the most northerly distillery in Scotland. The distillery is said to have been founded in 1798, but was not granted a license to distill until 1826. For the three intervening decades the distillery is said to have been run as an illicit operation by Magnus Eunson, one of Orkney's most infamous smugglers of the late eighteenth and early nineteenth centuries. Many different accounts detail Magnus's escapades and close scrapes with the law. Many make reference to him hiding his illicit whisky in the church; in one account he even faked a wake, hiding casks under a white sheet draped over a coffin lid in order to throw the law off his trail. When the distillery became licensed the days of smuggling were over, and for the next hundred years, although it had a few ups and downs, for the most part production was steady and the distillery grew.

The most notable change in ownership came in 1937, when the distillery was bought by Highland Distillers, now part of Edrington, current owner of Highland Park and several other distilleries. Under the guidance of Highland Distillers it prospered, and by the 1970s had become an established single-malt brand.

Over the decades the brand has grown considerably and has become one of the world's best-known and much-loved whiskies. The distillery still operates its own malting floor and makes a peated malt on site; this is supplemented with malt brought in from the mainland. The two malts are then combined to create a lightly peated spirit. Like The Macallan, Glenfarclas, and Glengoyne, Highland Park is a strong advocate of the sherry cask, spending millions each year in order to maintain a quality supply of sherry casks and retain Highland Park's character.

The Orkney Islands have a rich history, with Neolithic settlements dating back to around 3000 BCE and a strong Viking heritage. Inspired by this, the Highland Park brand team has released many Nordic themed whiskies. In 2012 the Valhalla series was launched, which to date features two limited releases called Thor and Loki (with two more to follow). This was followed by the launch of its Warrior series in 2013, which features six whiskies named after famous Vikings: Svein, Einar, Harald, Sigurd, Ragnvald, and Thorfinn. The main range features 12-, 15-, 18-, 21-, 25-, 30-, and 40-year-olds, and special and limited releases can also be found.

Thor

A mighty dram, with honeycomb and dense, spicy fruit on the nose, kicking spicy notes and fruit on the palate, and soft peat and licorice on the finish.

✴ ABV: 52.1% ✴ TYPE: Single Malt

12-Year-Old

A great all-round whisky and stepping stone into peated styles. Notes of heather, honey, and soft peat, fruit, spice, and soft smoke.

✴ ABV: 40% ✴ TYPE: Single Malt

18-Year-Old

Soft and spicy on the nose, with chocolate-covered raisins and sweet spice on the palate and soft peat on the finish.

✴ ABV: 43% ✴ TYPE: Single Malt

Talisker

The Talisker distillery is located on the Isle of Skye and was established in 1830 by two brothers local to the island called Hugh and Kenneth MacAskill. Skye is the largest island in the Inner Hebrides and draws thousands of tourists each year with its astounding natural beauty, but despite its size it has only the one distillery. Since its founding, Talisker, like most of Scotland's old distilleries, has had many different owners, not settling down until the 1930s, when it was acquired by a group of distillers called Scottish Malt Distillers (SMD). Over the decades SMD evolved into the drinks giant Diageo, which owns the distillery today. For the most part production at Talisker continued undisturbed until a major fire tore through the distillery in 1960. It was two years before the distillery was up and running again, as every piece of equipment had to be painstakingly remade in order not to alter the spirit style.

The distillery makes a peated style of whisky, which it produces using malted barley from the mainland and using five stills. Maturation takes place mainly in ex-bourbon casks, although sherry and port casks are also filled. The brand has been in the spotlight for quite some time since it joined the Classic Malts range in 1988, but compared to other classic malts the Talisker range is a bit bigger, with a handful of new releases emerging in 2013. The current range features Talisker 10- and 18-year-olds, Distillers Edition, 57° North, Storm, Darker Storm, and Port Ruighe (finished in port casks); older expressions include 25-, 27-, and most recently a 35-year-old.

18-Year-Old

Smoke, orange zest, oaky spice, and seaweed on the nose with soft peat, toffee, honey, and smoke on the palate and finish.

✴ ABV: 45.8% ✴ TYPE: Single Malt

Talisker Storm

Spicy, smoky, and coastal with notes of sweet peat, honey, smoke, and a peppery kick.

✴ ABV: 45.8% ✴ TYPE: Single Malt

Tobermory

The Tobermory distillery lies on the Isle of Mull off the west coast of Scotland on the edge of the small picturesque town of Tobermory, which is also the capital of the island. The town has a long history since being established as a fishing port in the late 1700s, and has a picturesque waterfront lined with houses painted in bright colors. It is probably best known (off the island and outside of Scotland) as the setting for the popular children's TV show *Balamory*.

The distillery is one of Scotland's oldest and was founded in 1798. Since its founding, the distillery has seen many periods of closure and many different owners. In 1993 the distillery was bought by Burn Stewart Distillers (owners of Bunnahabhain), which acquired the maturing stock in the deal. The distillery makes two types of spirit: lightly peated and heavily peated; the better-known is the lightly peated, which is sold under the name Tobermory, whereas the peated spirit is sold under the name Ledaig (pronounced *Le-chig*), meaning "safe haven" in Gaelic. The distillery is currently producing under its capacity, making around 200,000 gallons (750,000 liters) a year, around half of which is made using heavily peated malt brought in from Islay. Mainly American oak casks are filled, but some sherry casks are used, with the bulk of maturation taking place on the mainland. The current range features Tobermory 10- and 15-year-olds and Ledaig ten-year-old. In 2013 the range expanded with two distillery exclusive bottlings, a 19-year-old Tobermory and a 16-year-old Ledaig, both aged in Pedro Ximénez casks. A limited edition 40-year-old Ledaig can also be found.

Ledaig 10-Year-Old

Sweet and smoky on the nose with peat and light, fruity notes on the palate leading to a peppery, spicy, smoky finish.

✳ ABV: 46.3% ✳ TYPE: Single Malt

10-Year-Old

Light and citrusy on the nose with subtle earthy notes and toffee on the palate and finish.

✳ ABV: 46.3% ✳ TYPE: Single Malt

CAMBELTOWN

Long before Paul McCartney had heard of the Mull of Kintyre, the peninsula was famous for its whisky. Centered on Campbeltown, whisky production developed from the 1600s, thanks to plentiful supplies of barley and peat, and a remote location.

By 1794, 32 illicit stills were reportedly operating, but the Excise Act of 1823 made them legitimate concerns, and the town was soon producing 925,000 gallons (3.5 million liters) of spirit a year. Not for nothing did it become known as the whisky capital of the world.

An initial cornering of the Glasgow market had meant soaring demand for whisky; however, distillers could not keep up with demand and quality plummeted,

Campbeltown characteristics include a defined dryness with a pungency, smokiness, and solid salinity.

such that the whisky was sometimes referred to as "stinking fish." The fortunes of Campbeltown also took a downturn as its heavy whiskies fell out of favor, with blenders increasingly enamored with fragrant Speyside malts, while a further hammer-blow came with the introduction of Prohibition in the United States.

Most distilleries closed, and today only three remain in operation: namely Springbank, Glengyle, and Glen Scotia. However, quality control has been reasserted in those that remain.

Campbeltown characteristics include a defined dryness with a pungency, smokiness, and solid salinity. After years of being sidelined as a whisky region, Campbeltown is back with a vengeance.

Glengyle

Built in 1872, Glengyle, like so many other Campbeltown distilleries, faced closure in the 1920s, and in the years that followed it was converted into a gas station. It wasn't until 2000, when Glengyle was acquired by Springbank, that the distillery was rebuilt and reborn. The initiative is a family affair, as Springbank owner Hedley Wright is a descendant of the Mitchell family, who originally owned both businesses. Production began in 2004 and the first whisky is expected to be ready by 2014. Since another company was already using the name Glengyle for one of its blended malts, the distillery name could not be used so the name Kilkerran was chosen. The distillery is currently working at a fraction of its capacity, with around 7,900 gallons (30,000 liters) being produced in 2013. Expressions since 2007 have been labeled "Work in Progress," of which five are currently available.

Kilkerran Work in Progress Fifth Release— Sherry Wood

Rich and full of stewed and dried fruit flavors, this whisky shows great promise and in the years to come should evolve into a real gem.

★ ABV: 46% ★ Type: Single Malt

Glen Scotia

For nearly eight decades production at Glen Scotia has been sporadic at best. The distillery has had many owners throughout its life and has miraculously escaped permanent closure. It is rumored to be haunted by one of its previous owners, Duncan MacCallum. Duncan had previously saved the distillery from closure, but in 1928 it shut down after it hit significant financial issues, and two years later he drowned himself in the distillery's water source, Campbeltown Loch. Currently the future is looking brighter for Glen Scotia, and hopefully in the years to come it will start to grow out of the shadow of Springbank. The current owner has refurbished the distillery and launched a new range in late 2012, including 10-, 12-, 16-, 18-, and 21-year-olds.

Strawberry Ganache 1991, Wemyss Malts

This expression of Glen Scotia was bottled from a single cask by indie bottler Wemyss. Rich and full bodied, with notes of strawberry and cocoa alongside subtle smoke.

★ ABV: 46% ★ Type: Single Malt

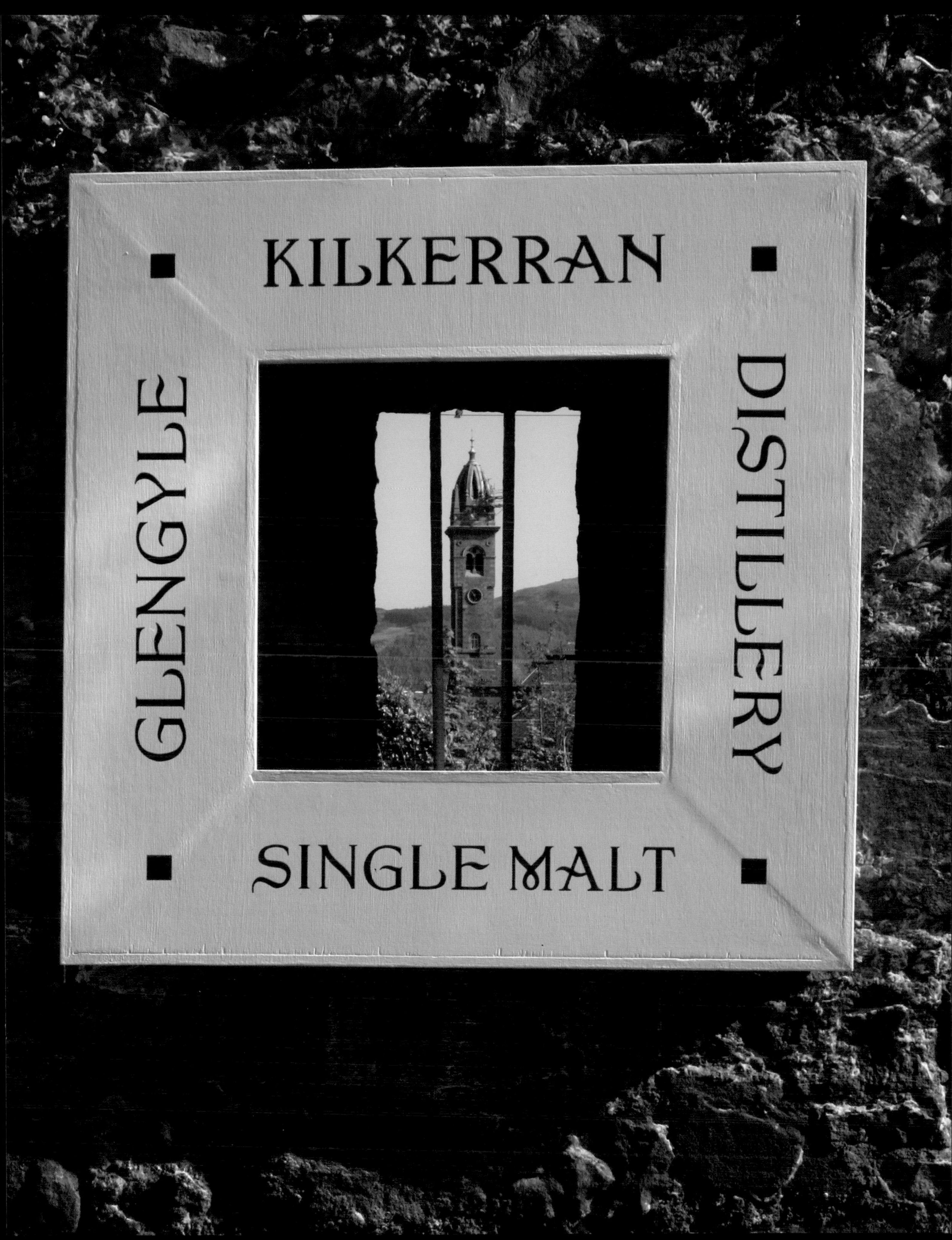
KILKERRAN
GLENGYLE
DISTILLERY
SINGLE MALT

Springbank

The Springbank distillery was founded in 1828 and is one of the few independently owned distilleries in Scotland, having remained under family ownership since its conception. The distillery sits in the center of Campbeltown, not far from the harbor where once thousands of casks would have been shipped to the United States. In its heyday Campbeltown had over 30 distilleries and was once known as the "whisky capital of the world." Today only three distilleries are working in Campbeltown, with Springbank and Glen Scotia being the only original survivors.

Springbank is unique among Scotland's distilleries in keeping production low and employing traditional methods throughout production. The distillery is one of only a handful that still malt their own barley on site, but unlike the others, Springbank's maltings service all the production requirements. This means production at Springbank is far lower than its potential capacity, only producing around 26,500 gallons (100,000 liters) of spirit a year. The distillery operates three stills: one wash still and two spirit stills. Unlike the spirit stills, which are heated by steam coils, the wash still is direct-fired using oil. Both the wash still and spirit still number two use tube condensers, whereas spirit still number one uses a worm tub to condense its spirit vapor.

The distillery produces three distinctly different whiskies: Springbank, Longrow, and Hazelburn, each with its own quirks in production. Springbank is the house style and is the main release, lightly peated and distilled two and a half times. Longrow is heavily peated and is distilled twice, while Hazelburn is totally unpeated and is triple distilled. Maturation takes place in number of different cask types, including ex-bourbon, sherry, and wine. Being family owned and independent, the distillery has been left to its own devices and has developed more organically than some bigger brands, and although demand is currently far outweighing supply, Springbank's methods don't budge. This approach is the antithesis to that of larger distilling companies, and for many old malt whisky fans provides the perfect antidote to other heavily marketed whiskies. Springbank's values, combined with some excellent whiskies, have helped elevate the distillery to a cultlike status with legions of avid fans around the world. The range features Springbank, 10-, 15-, and 18-year-olds, 12-year-old cask strength and a 21-year-old, Longrow NAS bottling, Longrow Red and 18-year-old, and Hazelburn 12-Year-Old. A number of limited releases and wood finishes can also be found.

10-Year-Old

Briny and thick with a heavy mouthfeel with notes of dried fruit, toffee, chocolate coated graham crackers and soft peat.

★ ABV: 46% ★ Type: Single Malt

Hazelburn 12-Year-Old

Rich and fruity but light in body with plenty of rich fruitcakey flavors, toffee, and chocolate raisins.

★ ABV: 46% ★ Type: Single Malt

Longrow

Sweet and smoky on the nose, with a soft creamy mouthfeel and notes of vanilla and oaky spice and peat throughout.

★ ABV: 46% ★ Type: Single Malt

The most expensive whiskies of all time

Whisky is for drinking, but as a scarce commodity, its value can make it a valuable investment opportunity, too. Rare bottles can sell for eye-popping figures, as this top ten shows:

1. A private Asian collector smashed the world record for whisky in January 2014 by paying H.K.$4.9 million (U.S.$632,000) for a The Macallan "M" Imperiale six-liter decanter by Lalique.
2. The previous record was also for The Macallan 1946 in a Lalique Cire Perdue decanter. It fetched $460,000 at a charity auction.
3. Only three bottles of Dalmore 64 Trinitas were made and one sold for $160,000 in 2010.
4. John Walker & Sons produced a limited edition of 60 bottles of Diamond Jubilee whisky to celebrate Queen Elizabeth II's anniversary in 2012. They cost $160,000 each.
5. A connoisseur from Atlanta, Georgia, bought a bottle of Glenfiddich Janet Sheed Roberts Reserve 1955 for $94,000.
6. One of only 40 bottles of The Macallan 1926 fetched $75,000 in 2005.
7. A blend of four Dalmore single malts called The Matheson was sold for $58,000 to a buyer who shared it with five friends.
8. Only 61 bottles of a Glenfiddich Rare Collection 1937 were produced. A charity auction in New York sold one for $20,000 in 2006.
9. Balvenie Cask 191 from 1952 produced 250 bottles, and there are still a few left for $13,000. Each is sealed with wax and hand-signed by the master distiller.
10. The Macallan again—a bottle of 55-year-old in a Lalique decanter will set you back $12,500.

SCOTTISH BLENDED AND GRAIN WHISKIES

Despite the growing appeal of malt whisky since the 1980s, blended whisky makes up more than 90 percent of the market. Most of the biggest and best-known Scotch whisky brands are blends, such as Johnnie Walker, Ballantine's, Famous Grouse, and Chivas Regal.

Blended whisky is created using a mix of malt and grain whiskies. The process was perfected from the mid-nineteenth century by pioneering figures such as Andrew Usher, Charles MacKinlay, and William Robertson.

Changes to the law permitting the mixing of whiskies opened the door to creating more palatable whisky with wider appeal. The malt whisky of the day could be fiery and downright nasty stuff. Blending allowed a more balanced product to emerge.

Most of the best-known blends of today date from this period, including Bell's (1851), Buchanan's (1884), Dewar's White Label (1899), Famous Grouse (1896), Teacher's Highland Cream (1884), Grant's (1898), and Vat 69 (1882).

There is no rule over the amount of malt and grain whisky in each blend and the composition of each is a closely guarded secret. There may be as many as 40 or 50 different malts in a blend, expertly put together by a master blender.

Grain whisky, long used as the cheap element in blends, is also experiencing a reinvention.

As malts have become more appreciated in recent years, blended whisky has sometimes been compared unfavorably. However, blends have fought back with more deluxe versions of old favorites designed to appeal to whisky drinkers looking for a more prestigious dram. Examples include Johnnie Walker Platinum, Famous Grouse's The Naked Grouse, and Grant's 25-year-old.

Grain whisky, long used as the cheap element in blends, is also experiencing a reinvention. William Grant & Sons is releasing single-grain whiskies in its Girvan Patent Still range. The 25-year-old and 30-year-old versions were launched at the decidedly upmarket price of $400 and $600 a bottle, respectively.

Ballantine's

The Ballantine's brand began in 1910, but it can trace its roots back to George Ballantine, who started selling whisky in his Edinburgh grocery store in 1827. George's business grew and in 1865 he set up another store in Glasgow. At this point George introduced his son, Archibald, to the business, and left him to run the Edinburgh enterprise while George took care of the new store in Glasgow. It was around this time that George began blending and creating his own whiskies.

As sales continued to grow, Ballantine brought another son into the fold, George Jr. In 1910 the brand Ballantine's was established and the company began exporting. In 1919 the brand was bought by entrepreneurs Jimmy Barclay and R. A. McKinlay, who began to establish it in the United States. Ballantine's continued to grow, and unlike its competitors, by the 1920s it was selling two older expressions: a 17- and a 30-year-old, which was certainly not the norm at the time. They were also ahead of the game in terms of

casks, utilizing a percentage of American white oak casks for maturation.

By the 1950s the brand was under the ownership of Hiram Walker–Gooderham & Worts, and was a huge success in the United States. Europe soon followed, and by the mid-1980s Ballantine's was the best-selling brand on the continent. Today the blend is under the ownership of Chivas, and can boast success in most markets, particularly Europe. The current range includes Finest, and 12-, 17-, 21-, 30- and 40-year-olds. Recently three limited expressions of different styles were introduced to emphasize three of the main constituent malts from Scapa, Miltonduff, and Glenburgie distilleries.

Finest

The best-selling whisky in the range and usually enjoyed with a mixer. Notes of heather, honey, candy apple, and oak.

★ ABV: 40% ★ Type: Scotch Blends

17-Year-Old

Soft and creamy with a fuller mouthfeel. Deep spicy notes combine with citrus, milk chocolate, vanilla, and subtle earthy peat.

★ ABV: 43% ★ Type: Scotch Blends

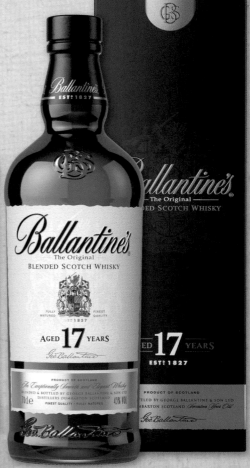

Black Bottle

In 1879 the three Graham brothers created and launched the Black Bottle blend. The whisky was bottled in a distinctive bottle from Germany made from black glass, which helped distinguish the blend from its various competitors. In 1914, when war broke out, this distinctive bottle, for obvious reasons, became impossible to get, so the whisky moved into a dumpy green bottle that is more familiar today. However, in 2013 the blend's owners decided to make a U-turn on this near century-old design and revert to the original black glass bottle used at the blend's inception. Until this relaunch Black Bottle claimed to contain whisky from every distillery on Islay (except Kilchoman), making it a far smokier tipple than most blends. The range currently consists of just the one whisky.

Black Bottle

Sweet, floral notes and gentle smoke on the nose, with fruit, heather, and honey on the palate leading to a soft, smoky finish.

✴ ABV: 40% ✴ TYPE: Scotch Blends

Bailie Nicol Jarvie (BNJ)

BNJ is among the blends most celebrated by whisky enthusiasts, as its high malt content and use of top-drawer grain whisky make it a more complex and challenging dram than other blends of a similar price. Made by the Glenmorangie Co., there's no doubting that it comprises some quality whiskies being put together by skilled blenders. The whisky takes its name from a well-known character in Walter Scott's novel *Rob Roy* and was very popular during the twentieth century. Although the whisky is widely available today, not much attention is paid to the brand, as the owners focus on their single malts Glenmorangie and Ardbeg. Aside from being a decent blend, BNJ is the perfect example of never judging a whisky by its label. The range consists of just the one whisky.

Blended Whisky

Lemon and lime hard candies, creamy vanilla and oak flavors balance perfectly leading to a spicy finish with a sherbetlike fizz.

✴ ABV: 40% ✴ TYPE: Scotch Blends

WHAT THEY SAY ...

"Ninety percent I'll spend on good times, women, and Irish whiskey. The other ten percent I'll probably waste."

——Tug McGraw

Chivas Regal

The story of Chivas begins in 1801 with the opening of a licensed grocery in Aberdeen by William Edward, who soon established a successful business as a purveyor of brandy, coffee, and spices to wealthy clients. In 1838 James Chivas joined the store as an assistant, eventually acquiring the business with a partner, Charles Stewart. In 1857 this partnership was dissolved and James partnered with his brother John, creating the company Chivas Brothers. The business continued to grow, and five years later, after John's death, James brought his son Alexander into the fold. By this time the company had already started to blend whiskies under a handful of names. Alexander continued to run the business until his death in 1893, after which the company passed to its clerk, Alexander J. Smith.

In 1909 the Chivas Regal brand was launched and soon became a hit in the United States, although like many other brands, this success was halted in 1920 by the introduction of Prohibition. In 1949 Seagram bought the brand and began to distribute the whisky widely, investing heavily in advertizing and infrastructure. It also purchased the Strathisla distillery, which was (and still is) the source of the key malt needed to make the Chivas blend. During the 1950s the brand was relaunched in the United States and took the country by storm, becoming the whisky of choice for a number of celebrities, including Frank Sinatra. Today the whisky is the second best-selling premium blended whisky in the world and the best seller in Southeast Asia and Europe. The range features 12-, 18-, and 25-year-olds.

12-Year-Old

A well-rounded, easygoing blend with notes of honey, mixed fruit, vanilla, and soft spice.

✴ ABV: 40% ✴ TYPE: Scotch Blends

18-Year-Old

Dried fruit and toffee on the nose, with dark chocolate and marmalade on the palate leading to a sweet, slightly smoky finish.

✴ ABV: 40% ✴ TYPE: Scotch Blends

Cutty Sark

Cutty Sark was conceived in 1923 and has grown to be one of the best-selling whiskies in the United States and indeed in the world. The whisky takes its name from the famous British tea clipper that was launched in 1869 and was the fastest ship of her day. She rode the waves until 1954, when she was dry-docked in Greenwich, London. The ship is the only surviving extreme clipper and was the highest development of the fast commercial sailing ship. She survives today as a major tourist attraction and receives thousands of visitors each year. Interestingly, the ship took its name from a young witch, who wore a "cutty sark" (short nightdress) in the famous poem *Tam O'Shanter* by Robert Burns.

The blend was radical in its day as its creators, Berry Bros. & Rudd, decided to focus on a lighter style aimed at the American market. This pale-colored whisky with its lighter flavors must have been a real breath of fresh air on the whisky scene of the 1920s, when most blends would have been dark and rich. The blend was under the ownership of Berry's until 2010, when it joined the Edrington portfolio alongside whiskies such as Famous Grouse and Highland Park. Edrington had been behind the production of the blend for many years and was the ideal candidate to take it forward and revive sales, which had been decreasing. The range includes the standard bottling, Storm, Prohibition Edition, 15- and 18-year-olds, and the 25-year-old Tam O'Shanter.

Cutty Sark

Perfect whisky for hotter climes. Light, clean, and fresh, with notes of citrus, sweet cereal, vanilla, and honey.

★ ABV: 40% ★ Type: Scotch Blends

Prohibition Edition

A far punchier version with more weight, grip, and complexity. Notes of citrus, pepper, dark toffee, vanilla, and slightly burned granola.

★ ABV: 50% ★ Type: Scotch Blends

Dewar's

In 1846 John Dewar, a wine and spirit merchant from Perth, created the very first Dewar's blend. Little did he know that the creation of this whisky would build an empire and that it would become one of the top ten best-selling blended whiskies in the world. When he died in 1880 the business was handed to his two sons, John Alexander and Tommy, who set to work growing the brand into the giant we know today. Through their ingenuity the brothers propelled Dewar's onto the international stage, and began to reap the rewards of what was a very lucrative time for the whisky industry. In 1898 the two brothers set about building the Aberfeldy distillery, which to this day remains the spiritual home of the Dewar's blend. The Dewar's core range includes White Label, 12-, 15-, and 18-year-olds, and the De Luxe Signature.

White Label

Once marketed in early advertisements as the whisky that never varies. A honeyed sweetness balanced with notes of heather and oak.

✴ ABV: 40% ✴ TYPE: Scotch Blends

Haig Dimple

The Haig family are rooted deep in the history of Scotch whisky distilling, with Robert Haig being recorded as a distiller in 1655. Nearly 200 years later, in 1824, John Haig, the direct descendant of Robert, built the Cameron Bridge distillery in the Lowlands. The distillery was one of the first to make grain whisky and used some of the first column stills, invented by John's cousin, Richard Stein. This type of still was the latest in distillation technology, and toward the end of the nineteenth century would change the face of whisky forever. The Dimple brand, known as Pinch in the United States, came about soon after Cameron Bridge was built, and with its distinctive bottle is one of the most iconic whiskies ever made.

Dimple 15-Year-Old

A sweet, buttery nose with caramel, poached pears, and cakey spice on the palate. The finish is soft with a trace of dark chocolate.

✴ ABV:40% ✴ TYPE: Scotch Blends

Famous Grouse

The Famous Grouse can trace its roots right back to the 1820s, when the Gloag family started a licensed grocery in Perth. The business was originally focused on wine but was steered toward whisky in 1860 when the business passed to William Gloag after the death of his father, and continued with the support of his nephew, Matthew. It was in 1896, a year after William's death, that the Grouse brand was born, becoming Famous Grouse in 1905. The "Famous" was added as a reflection of its growing popularity, especially with the tourist trade at the time, which consisted mainly of sports hunters and fishermen.

One of the main differences between Famous Grouse and other whiskies of the era was the marketing strategy. While most companies were striving to take advantage of the American market, the Gloags focused on selling locally and rarely sold outside Scotland. The business remained in family hands until 1970, when it was sold to Edrington. Under its wing the brand grew rapidly, becoming the best-selling whisky in Scotland and one of the world's best-selling blends. The Glenturret distillery, also owned by Edrington, plays a vital role in the whisky as it provides a key malt whisky used in the blend, so much so that the distillery is also known as the Famous Grouse Experience. The current range features the standard Famous Grouse, Black Grouse (peated), Snow Grouse (grain whisky), and Naked Grouse. Numerous limited and special releases can be found.

Famous Grouse

....

A good quality and versatile blend with notes of chocolate orange, citrus, caramel, and vanilla.

★ ABV: 40% ★ TYPE: Scotch Blends

Naked Grouse

....

A malt-heavy blend aged in first-fill sherry casks. Incredibly soft and creamy, with notes of dried fruit, grape juice, cinnamon, and oaky spice.

★ ABV: 40% ★ TYPE: Scotch Blends

Grant's

The Grant's blend was introduced around the turn of the nineteenth century, in the years following the founding of the Glenfiddich distillery by William Grant, who began working with whisky at a young age at the Mortlach distillery. After working his way up through the ranks William became manager, and after 20 years at Mortlach he set about building his own distillery, Glenfiddich, in 1887. In the following years William, together with his sons, set about establishing what would eventually grow to be one of the best-selling blends in the world. In 1909 William's son-in-law, Charles Gordon, became one of the company's first salesmen, ensuring sales of the whisky in the Far East, while John Grant brokered deals in the West.

The combined efforts of the Grant's team in these early years meant that by the early 1900s their whisky was available in many countries around the world. In 1957 they further differentiated themselves from the competition when they adopted the iconic triangular bottle designed for them by Hans Schleger, also used for Glenfiddich single malt whisky a couple of years later. The Grant's blend contains malt whisky from Kininvie and grain whisky from the company's enormous Girvan distillery in Ayrshire. William Grant & Sons remains a family-run business to this day. The Grant's range features the Family Reserve, Ale Cask Finish, Sherry Cask Finish, 12-, 18-, and 25-year-olds.

25-Year-Old

Fruit salad and sherry trifle on the nose, with spicy oak and baked apple on the palate and a spicy, woody finish.

✴ ABV: 40% ✴ TYPE: Scotch Blends

Ale Cask Finish

The ale casks add an interesting layer of extra flavor. Sweet and approachable, with notes of diced green fruit and crème brûlée.

✴ ABV: 40% ✴ TYPE: Scotch Blends

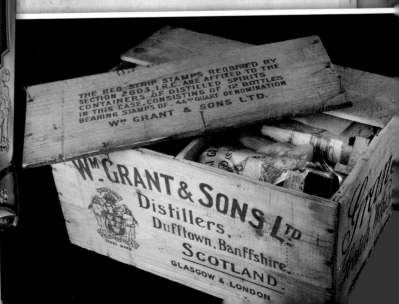

Hankey Bannister

Beaumont Hankey and Hugh Bannister started out in 1757 as London-based wine and spirit merchants. It wasn't until the 1800s that the duo embarked on making their own whisky, which, thanks to a shift in popular culture at the time (partly down to Queen Victoria's love of all things Scottish), soon gained traction and began to make a name for itself among the London gentry. These days the brand is owned by Inver House Distillers, owner of Old Pulteney, Knockdhu, Speyburn, and Balmenach distilleries, and is still a popular blend, sold in over 40 countries worldwide. Hankey Bannister has been the favorite tipple of many British royals and was given a royal warrant under King George V; it was also a favorite of wartime Prime Minister Winston Churchill. The range currently consists of the Original, Heritage, 12-, 21-, 25-, and 40-year-olds.

12-Year-Old

A light and slightly cagey nose, traces of fudge, black pepper on the palate, with a well-rounded and fruity finish.

✷ ABV: 40% ✷ Type: Scotch Blends

Isle of Skye

The Isle of Skye blend is owned and produced by Ian Macleod Distillers, owner of the Glengoyne distillery, and one of the largest independent family-owned companies in the spirits industry. The blend is a little punchier than most, as a good proportion of its malts are of the peated variety. At one stage the blend may have contained whisky from Talisker (the only distillery on Skye), though these days this is less likely. That said, it still has a bold character, appealing to those with a preference toward a bolder, smokier blend. The range starts with an eight-year-old, every drop of which has been aged for a minimum of eight years, setting it aside from other blends of a similar price, which seem to have lost their age statements over the last few years.

Isle of Skye Eight-Year-Old

Notes of buttercream frosting and smoke on the nose. The palate is full with rich fruit, honeycomb, and peat leading to a sweet, spicy finale.

✷ ABV: 40% ✷ Type: Scotch Blends

J&B

The story of this world-famous blend began in 1749, when an Italian by the name of Giacomo Justerini came to London in pursuit of an Italian opera singer called Margherita Bellino. Unfortunately for Giacomo, the young singer wasn't interested, but his journey was not in vain as he remained in London and set up the company that would eventually (long after his death) make one of the world's best-selling blended whiskies. In 1830 Alfred Brooks bought the business and changed the business name to the current version—Justerini & Brooks. It wasn't until the 1930s that the J&B we know today was first created, and, thanks to some well-cultivated connections in the United States, following the end of Prohibition in 1933, J&B was set to take America by storm—and the rest of the world soon after.

J&B Rare

A light nose with a trace of citrus and oak. Toffee and a nutty flavor emerge on the palate, followed by a clean and fresh finish.

★ ABV: 40% ★ Type: Scotch Blends

Tweeddale

The Tweeddale blend was first made in 1820 by a company called J. & A. Davidson. In the year 1895 it employed a young lad called Richard Day, who after years of learning the skills of whisky blending, would take over the company in 1923. In the years leading up to World War II, the production of the Tweeddale blend stopped, and after the war Richard set about selling off any remaining casks and the whisky was lost. This was until Alasdair Day, great-grandson of Richard, inherited his great-grandfather's cellar book, which contained the recipe for the forgotten blend. Alasdair began work reconstructing the whisky and in 2010 released the first batch of Tweeddale in over 70 years. Unlike other blends, the Tweeddale is made in small batches with only a handful of casks used each time.

Batch Four

Notes of toffee, honey, tropical fruits, cream soda, cocoa, soft peat, and vanilla combine to create a complex and rewarding whisky.

★ ABV: 46% ★ Type: Scotch Blends

WHAT THEY SAY ...

"No married man is genuinely happy if he has to drink worse whisky than he used to drink when he was single."

——H. L. Mencken

Johnnie Walker

The Johnnie Walker brand is arguably the most successful whisky ever created, and since World War II has been the best-selling whisky in the world. It can trace its beginnings to 1805 with the birth of John (Johnnie) Walker at Todriggs Farm near Kilmarnock. When John was 14, his father died and the family farm was sold, with the proceeds of £537.15 (around $2,000) being left to John. The money was used to invest in a small grocery store in Kilmarnock, which within a few years became a successful business and sold, among many other things, whisky.

In 1860 a significant law was passed in Scotland that allowed for the mixing of malt and grain whiskies, and began a revolution in Scotch whisky. By this point John's son, Alexander, was involved in the business and quickly set to work to capitalize on the new opportunity. By 1877 he had registered the Johnnie Walker label, which became known as the signature of Walker's Old Highland Whisky, while around 1860 he had started to use the rectangular bottle that is still in use today. As the years went by, the brand expanded and its appeal spread; by the 1880s it was the best-selling whisky in Sydney and a few years later in South

Africa, too. Demand was growing and so, too, was the business, and in 1893 steps were taken to ensure a steady supply of malt whisky with the purchase of the Cardhu distillery. In 1889, when Alexander died, the business had passed to the next generation of Walkers, Alexander II and George.

The pair continued to grow the business, and in 1909 revised and renamed their range, creating the Red and Black Labels we know today. The previous year also saw the introduction of the famous Striding Man, created by cartoonist Tom Browne. In 1925 the company merged with several others, creating the infamous Distillers Company Ltd. (DCL); this was the beginning of the giant drinks company Diageo, which owns the brand today. In the years following the merger the brand continued to expand, receiving a royal warrant in 1934 and the Queen's Award for Export Achievement in 1966. The range today features the number-one best-selling whisky in the world, Red Label, together with Black Label, Double Black, Gold Label Reserve, Platinum Label, and Blue Label. Many limited and commemorative releases can be found, as well as the discontinued Green Label.

Platinum Label 18-Year-Old

The latest addition to the range. Notes of rhubarb crumble with vanilla custard, sweet spice, milk chocolate, and subtle smoke.

★ ABV: 40% ★ Type: Scotch Blends

Black Label 12-Year-Old

One of the best blends available. Fruit and spice on the nose, with toffee and soft smoke on the palate and finish.

★ ABV: 40% ★ Type: Scotch Blends

Double Black

Made with a higher percentage of peated whisky. Sweet smoke on the nose and candy apple, vanilla, peat, and oaky spice.

★ ABV: 40% ★ Type: Scotch Blends

Vat 69

The Vat 69 blend takes its unusual name from an experiment in 1882 conducted by its creator, William Sanderson. In his quest to create the best blend he could, he invited around 100 of his friends to form a panel of judges and try 100 different blends, or "vattings" as they were known then, which he had made. The panel voted Vat 69 the best and the brand was born ... or so the story goes. True or not, the blend has been a success and was apparently a favorite of explorer Sir Ernest Shackleton, who took supplies of the whisky on his Imperial Trans-Antarctic Expedition in 1914. These days the blend forms part of the Diageo portfolio and is mainly targeted at markets in Venezuela, Spain, and Australia.

Vat 69

Hints of citrus, some oak, and traces of fruit and vanilla. A simple whisky usually accompanied with a mixer.

✹ ABV: 40% ✹ Type: Scotch Blends

White Horse

The earliest reference to White Horse is from 1880, when owner Peter Jeffery Mackie registered the name as a trademark in the United Kingdom; however, it is possible that White Horse was being made and sold prior to this date. The whisky takes its name from what was the famous White Horse Cellar Inn in Edinburgh. Unlike the vast majority of blends, White Horse has a slightly peaty character, which comes from its backbone malt, Lagavulin. How much of this iconic Islay malt is in the blend today is questionable, but it is still said to have a 40 percent malt content, which is significantly higher than other blends. White Horse can be found in most countries and has always been a popular and well-priced blend. The core range consists of the standard and a 12-year-old version.

White Horse

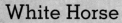

Fresh green fruit, honey, and vanilla combine with smoke, peat, and earthy flavors. A fantastic value and complex blend.

✹ ABV: 40% ✹ Type: Scotch Blends

Whyte & Mackay

James Whyte and Charles Mackay began their journey into the whisky trade in the latter half of the 1800s while working for a company called Allan and Poynter, which operated a dry-goods warehouse in Glasgow. When the business owner died, the company was sold to James and Charles, who renamed it Whyte & Mackay. Soon afterward they bought a new facility in Glasgow and began blending and bottling their own whisky. Owing to a number of collapses in the industry and the two world wars, it wasn't until the 1950s and 1960s that Whyte & Mackay whisky really took off. In 1960 Whyte & Mackay bought The Dalmore distillery, followed by Fettercairn in 1973. The range consists of Special, 13-Year-Old, Old Luxury, Supreme, and 30-Year-Old.

The Thirteen

Rich fruit and spice on the nose. The palate is soft and weighty, delivering fruit and honey followed by a decent firm finish.

★ ABV: 40% ★ Type: Scotch Blends

WHAT THEY SAY …

"There is no such thing as bad whiskey. Some whiskeys just happen to be better than others. But a man shouldn't fool with booze until he's fifty; then he's a damn fool if he doesn't."

—William Faulkner

Top ten blends

Despite the fact that malt whisky often gets most of the praise from critics and whisky snobs, blended whisky accounts for more than 90 percent of sales. Some drinkers prefer the fact that a great blend is a more balanced drink, and sales around the world appear to back this up.

Blends are typically a mix of 60 percent grain whisky and 40 percent malt, although the precise mix remains a secret of each producer. Likewise the exact type of whisky that goes into a blend is a matter of conjecture. A blend can contain up to 50 different malts as the master blender tries to create a perfect and consistent flavor profile.

The top ten Scotch whisky brands for 2012 were all blends:

1. Johnnie Walker—19.7 million cases (Diageo)
2. Ballantine's—5.8 million cases (Pernod Ricard)
3. Chivas Regal—4.8 million cases (Pernod Ricard)
4. J&B Rare—4.6 million cases (Diageo)
5. William Grant's—4.5 million cases (William Grant & Sons)
6. The Famous Grouse—3.2 million cases (Edrington)
7. Dewar's—3 million cases (Bacardi)
8. William Lawson's—2.6 million cases (Bacardi)
9. Label 5—2.5 million cases (La Martiniquaise)
10. Bell's—2.5 million cases (Diageo)

(Source: The Drinks Business)

Big Peat

Big Peat arrived on the shelves of whisky specialists in the fall of 2009 and was soon a hit with whisky drinkers, who enjoyed a big whisky full of smoky and peaty character, and also with those who didn't take their whisky too seriously. Despite Big Peat's comic appearance it includes some pretty impressive whiskies, such as Port Ellen, from a now-closed Islay distillery. Bottlings of Port Ellen can sell for thousands of dollars these days, so this move by Douglas Laing was an interesting one and certainly created a buzz around the whisky world. As with all the whiskies from Douglas Laing, no coloring is added to Big Peat, so the color of the whisky can vary slightly from batch to batch. This is viewed by many specialists as a positive. Big Peat has a festive counterpart bottled at cask strength.

Big Peat

As expected, peat and smoke dominate the nose, palate, and finish, but subtle citrus and traces of mixed fruit and salted nuts twist and turn in the fore.

★ ABV: 46% ★ Type: Blended Malt

Blue Hanger

Created by Berry Bros. & Rudd and named after one of their favorite customers of the late seventeenth century. The illustrious and fashionable William Hanger, third Lord Coleraine, acquired the nickname "Blue Hanger" as he was partial to wearing lots of blue clothes. The whisky is made in small batches, with only a few thousand bottles available at a time. Only a handful of casks are used in each batch and are normally a combination of ex-bourbon and sherry casks. It's rumored that Blue Hanger was a favorite of the British military and was issued to British spies during the two world wars. Berry Bros. have been filling the spirit cellars and cabinets of the British aristocracy for three centuries and carry two royal warrants.

9th Limited Release

Orange peel, vanilla, peat, and soft smoke wrapped in a rich, weighty mouthfeel. This release carries more peat and less sherry influence than other batches.

★ ABV: 45.6% ★ Type: Blended Malt

Compass Box

Compass Box Whisky Company was set up at the turn of the twenty-first century by whisky maker John Glaser and produces a collection of unusual blended malts and blends. John learned the art of whisky blending with one of the biggest whisky companies, and since starting Compass Box has put those skills to good use creating an innovative and diverse array of whiskies. Oak Cross is made from three Highland single malts, which have been matured partially in bespoke casks made of both American and new French oak.

As with many independent whisky companies, Compass Box doesn't chill-filter and no coloring is added to its whiskies. The range includes three blended malts, namely Oak Cross, Spice Tree, and Peat Monster, the blended Asyla, an experimental blend called Great King Street, and the grain whisky Hedonism.

Hedonism is one of very few available examples of blended grain whisky. Between eight and ten casks are married together to form this great example of the type. The whiskies used to create Hedonism can vary in origin, but are usually sourced from Cameron Bridge, Carsebridge, Cambus, Port Dundas, and Dumbarton distilleries. A combination of American oak hogshead casks and first-fill bourbon casks are used in maturation and transform the light grain spirits into a rich, soft bourbonesque style of whisky. Other expressions of Hedonism have included Hedonism Maximus, a limited release using grain whiskies up to 42 years old, and a 38-year-old Invergordon limited to 120 bottles to celebrate Compass Box's tenth anniversary.

Hedonism

Sweet vanilla and buttery popcorn on the nose, with toffee, vanilla, and cocoa on the palate followed by a clean, spicy finish.

★ ABV: 46% ★ TYPE: Grain

Oak Cross

Aromas of woody spice, vanilla, and citrus appear on the nose, with notes of dried fruits and cinnamon on the palate, culminating in a sweet woody finish.

★ ABV: 43% ★ TYPE: Blended Malt

Mackinlay's

In 1907 British explorer Ernest Shackleton set off on an expedition to the South Pole, and to help the team on its arduous journey, 25 cases of Mackinlay's whisky were loaded up along with the other essential supplies. Although they never reached the South Pole, the expedition did eventually result in what is probably the greatest whisky discovery of modern times, when in 2007 three cases of Mackinlay's whisky were found beneath the expedition hut. The whisky had been encased in ice for a century and was almost perfectly preserved, offering a window into the whisky of yesteryear. After careful analysis by Whyte & Mackay (owners of Mackinlay), the whisky was recreated and released in 2011, to be followed by a second release in early 2013.

Shackleton Rare Old Highland Malt Journey Edition

Baked apple with vanilla and a whiff of smoke on the nose, followed by stewed fruit and orange zest on the palate, with subtle peat toward the end.

✽ ABV: 47.3% ✽ TYPE: Blended Malt

The sweet sound of collaboration

Malt whisky is associated with the finer things in life, so it was perhaps no surprise when Orkney-based Highland Park partnered with the maker of some of the world's most elite sound systems, Linn.

In 2013 the Scottish company had been producing its pricey hi-fi decks for 40 years, and hit on a suitably exclusive way of celebrating the fact when it created 40 limited-edition turntables using wood sourced from Highland Park barrels.

Costing a cool $42,000 each, the turntables come complete with a special $1,500 bottle of Highland Park 40-year-old with which to relax, recline, and listen to your favorite record. The plinth of the iconic Sondek LP12 turntable, the product on which the company was founded, is crafted from the solid oak casks used to mature Highland Park's award-winning whisky.

As well as both companies being Scottish success stories, they are renowned for their attention to detail and commitment to quality. Linn is famous for designing and making the best music systems in the world, producing everything in-house at its factory just outside Glasgow. Highland Park has a similarly obsessive reputation, and is one of the few distilleries that still malts its own barley by hand.

Other whiskies are also partnering with luxury brands to create marketing synergies. The Dalmore has enjoyed a number of such links in recent years, including with Lutwyche handmade shoes, Harrods Fine Spirits Room, and upmarket property developer Finchatton. The latter deal treated the purchaser of a $25–30 million penthouse apartment in Mayfair, London, to a one-off bottle of vintage Dalmore produced by the company's master distiller.

Monkey Shoulder

Created by William Grant & Sons, Monkey Shoulder is made using malt whisky from the company's three Speyside distilleries, namely Glenfiddich, The Balvenie, and the lesser-known Kininvie distillery. Kininvie is not readily available as a single malt, since the distillery was built in the 1990s to help take the pressure off Balvenie and Glenfiddich and produce malt whisky for the Grant's blend. It has only been released a couple of times, under the name Hazelwood, making opportunities to try it next to impossible. Monkey Shoulder takes its unusual name from an affliction suffered by the maltmen of yesteryear, when the turning of hundreds of tons of malt by hand caused their arms to hang down like a monkey's. The whisky was first launched in 2005 and has helped bring the blended malt category into the mainstream.

Monkey Shoulder

Banana and custard on the nose, with mixed fruit and hard candy on the palate, leading to a pleasant finish of vanilla and oak.

★ ABV: 40% ★ Type: Blended Malt

The Six Isles

The Six Isles is a unique whisky made using malts from six of the seven whisky-producing islands of Scotland. Whiskies from Arran, Islay, Jura, Mull, Skye, and Orkney are matured in American oak and married to create a whisky of interesting balance and complexity. It doesn't take much detective work to identify the distilleries of origin, since Arran, Jura, Mull, and Skye only have one distillery each, and a clue on the label gives an indication of which of the Orkney distilleries is involved. However, the Islay distillery remains a mystery. The Six Isles belongs to Ian Macleod Distillers, owners of the Glengoyne distillery and a number of other brands, including the Isle of Skye blend. A limited release of The Six Isles, finished in Pomerol wine casks, was released in 2010.

The Six Isles

Soft smoke, sea spray, and peat on the nose. The palate opens up, with vanilla, fruit, and peaty flavors followed by a short, sweet finish.

★ ABV: 40% ★ Type: Blended Malt

Cameron Brig

The Cameronbridge Distillery was founded by John Haig in 1824, and was the first distillery in Scotland to produce grain whisky. The distillery used some of the very first column stills, which were designed by John's cousin, Richard Stein. The distillery is enormous and dwarfs even the largest malt whisky distilleries, with an estimated annual production of well over 26.5 million gallons (100 million liters) of spirit. It has long been under the ownership of Diageo and plays a key role in the company. Several different spirits have their origins at Cameronbridge, including Smirnoff Vodka and Gordon's Gin. The Cameron Brig range consists of just the one whisky, although a 25-year-old limited edition was made available in 1999 to commemorate the 175th anniversary of John receiving his license to distill. A handful of independent bottlings can also be found.

Cameron Brig

Light, easygoing, and uncomplicated with subtle traces of honey, vanilla, and dried fruit.

✶ ABV: 40% ✶ TYPE: Grain

Girvan

The Girvan distillery was built in 1963 by William Grant & Sons and is a giant distillery capable of producing 28.3 million gallons (107 million liters) a year. The Girvan site is enormous, boasting its own cooperage and 42 warehouses, with another 30 due to be built in the coming years. Until 2013 the only way you could try Girvan was through an independent bottling, but late that year the distillery released an official range of Girvans, which include a no-age-statement bottling, a 25-year-old, and a 30-year-old. Around half of Girvan's production is sold to other companies and the rest is mainly used in the Grant's blend. Independent bottlings are numerous and can be found in specialist stores. This particular release was bottled by Douglas Laing, one of the larger independent bottlers. Its grain whiskies are released under the Clan Denny name.

The Clan Denny 1965, 46-Year-Old

Rich and sweet on the nose, with apple strudel and vanilla ice cream on the palate, followed by a sweet, spicy finish.

✶ ABV: 49.7% ✶ TYPE: Blended Malt

Invergordon

The Invergordon distillery was founded in 1959 on the shores of the Cromarty Firth, north of Inverness. Invergordon is the only grain distillery in the Highlands of Scotland and is not far from the Dalmore distillery. The distillery was built by Invergordon Distillers Ltd., and for a short time it was home to the Ben Wyvis distillery. Ben Wyvis was built within the Invergordon complex in 1965 in order to contribute malt whisky to Whyte & Mackay, but was demolished after only 11 years in 1977. Although not well known, bottlings of Ben Wyvis are incredibly rare and highly collectable. Invergordon Distillers Ltd. was eventually absorbed by Whyte & Mackay in 1993 and the whisky is still used in its blends today. Independent bottlings of Invergordon are numerous and can be great value for money.

Berry Bros. & Rudd
Invergordon 1988, cask #8997

Soft oak and vanilla on the nose with chocolate ice cream and honey on the palate and a long, buttery finish.

★ ABV: 46% ★ TYPE: Grain

IRELAND

The Irish like to boast that they were the first to distill whiskey and that they shared the knowledge with their Scottish neighbors across the Irish Sea.

If this is the case, they didn't make the most of their advantage, for it was Scotch whisky that went on to conquer the world, while the Irish variant has had a tougher time. That was certainly the case until recently. Irish whiskey may be the smallest of the "big four" of Scotch, bourbon, Canadian, and Irish, but it is now the fastest growing of them all. It is also outstripping any other spirits category globally.

Irish whiskey must be made in Ireland and the Irish spell it "whiskey," whereas the Scots drop the "e." It is typically a triple-distilled spirit in contrast to the twice-distilled Scotch, using unpeated malt. Like Scotch, Irish whiskey is aged in wooden casks for a minimum of three years. The absence of peat in most of the better-known Irish whiskeys, combined with triple distillation, produces a smooth texture and a fruity profile in the final spirit.

Another important difference is the Irish use of unmalted as well as malted barley in the distillation process. The main flavor of Irish whiskey, like any other, comes from the cask. But the use of unmalted barley in the process creates its unique style.

History has it that distilling was occurring in Ireland as early as the sixth century. At any rate, by the sixteenth century, whiskey was being produced by religious orders for consumption by the privileged. Elizabeth I was reportedly fond of Irish whiskey, as was Peter the Great of Russia.

Home distilling was common prior to the Tudor settlement of Ireland, but in 1608 the state began to issue licenses for distilling. Among the first to be granted was a license for Antrim governor Sir Thomas Phillips to distill in the Bushmills region. The 1608 date is still printed on the labels of Bushmills whiskey, and Bushmills Distillery claims to be the oldest licensed distillery in the world.

By the late eighteenth century, about 2,000 stills were in operation, most of them illegal. When Victorian historian Alfred Barnard visited Ireland in 1885, researching his book *The Whisky Distilleries of the United Kingdom*, there were only 28 legal distillers.

However, at the time Irish whiskey was considered the best in the world and the "Big Four" Dublin distilleries of John Jameson & Son, John Power & Son, George Roe & Co., and William Jameson & Co. had

a combined output of five million gallons per year. By contrast Scotland's distilleries were piddling affairs, with an average production of 100,000 gallons.

This would prove to be a high watermark for Irish whiskey. The patent still may have been perfected by an Irishman, Aeneas Coffey, but Irish distillers stuck to their pot stills, while the Scots eagerly adapted the more efficient means of distilling, which proved to be a crucial element in the ongoing success of blended Scotch. Meanwhile, the institution of the Irish Free State in 1922 led to trade embargoes that

shut off the Irish distillers' main market in Britain and its empire. Even large companies had to scale back production—to just two weeks per year in the 1930s in the case of the Old Midleton Distillery. At the same time the coming of Prohibition in 1920 in the United States closed off the primary export market and proved a mortal blow to many small distillers. Many of the remaining distillers were then caught out by the repeal of Prohibition and were insufficiently stocked.

Distillers Jameson, Power, and Cork survived by consolidation, forming the Irish Distillers Group in 1966. They gradually closed their old sites and moved production to a new state-of-the-art plant in Midleton. In the early 1970s they also acquired the Old Bushmills Distillery. At this low point production was probably down to fewer than 500,000 cases a year.

However, from here the comeback started. In 1987 the first new Irish distillery for over a century appeared when the independent Cooley Distillery was founded by John Teeling in Riverstown near Dundalk. Whiskeys such as Kilbeggan, Connemara, and Tyrconnell have been lauded, and the company was bought by Jim Beam in 2011.

> Irish whiskey is typically a triple-distilled spirit in contrast to the twice-distilled Scotch, using unpeated malt.

At the same time, other spirits players such as Diageo, William Grant, and Illva Saronno woke up to the possibilities for Irish whiskey and started to put money and marketing effort behind their brands. Suddenly Irish whiskey was sexy. The result has been two decades of steady growth, with sales building to 6.5 million cases in 2013. Expansion of 20 percent a year is anticipated, resulting in €400 million ($550 million) of planned investment in new production facilities in the next few years.

It's not just the big players that are benefiting. Dingle Distillery opened in May 2013 as a craft producer of artisan whiskey. It plans to produce whiskeys called Dingle Gold and Dingle Green, with projected output of two casks per day. As a promotion to attract investors it is offering 500 special casks, to be ready in 2018, to whiskey enthusiasts, who will earn the title of a "Founding Father of Dingle."

Niche Drinks is building a $25 million distillery in Derry to produce whiskey and liqueurs. The city was once the biggest producer of whiskey in the world. Meanwhile, Walsh Whiskey Distillery is investing €25 million ($35 million) in expanding the operations for its brands, which include The Irishman and Writers Tears.

It all adds up to a picture of renewed vigor and greater variety for the Irish whiskey industry.

Bushmills

Bushmills distillery resides in County Antrim in Northern Ireland, not far from the famous landmark, the Giant's Causeway. The distillery was founded in 1784, which places Bushmills among the oldest whiskey distilleries in the world. However, an interesting quirk is that the site on which the distillery was built was first granted a license to distill whiskey in 1608 by King James I. Today Bushmills is the second best-selling Irish whiskey, but this was not always the case, and like all the old Irish whiskey brands and companies, Bushmills has had to endure many times of hardship over the decades. Among these was a fire that occurred in 1885, destroying most of the distillery, and although it was soon rebuilt and bounced back, another disaster loomed in the not-too-distant future.

In the early 1900s the demise of the Irish whiskey industry started to set in. This period was caused by a combination of events, but two of the major contributors were the Irish War of Independence and Prohibition in the United States. This period saw the downfall of dozens of distilleries, and the extinction of hundreds of Irish whiskey brands. However, Bushmills weathered these tough times and like Jameson, Midleton, Powers, and a handful of others, it pulled through. But the dark times didn't stop there; during World War II the distillery was forced to stop making whiskey, and the company's archive in its head office was destroyed during an air raid by the German Luftwaffe.

Thankfully, the dark days of Irish whiskey did end, and now the whole category is seeing a revival. In recent years the distillery has seen huge investment by owner Diageo and rapid growth in sales worldwide. Unlike Ireland's other large distilleries, Midleton and Cooley, Bushmills only produces malt whiskey, which it triple-distills in traditional copper pot stills. Since Bushmills does not have column stills, it buys in its grain whiskey from Midleton in order to produce the distillery's blends. The Bushmills single malt whiskeys consist of 10-, 16-, and 21-year-old single malts; these are accompanied by the two core blends: Bushmills Original and Black Bush. Numerous limited releases have been available over the years, as well as a 12-year-old distillery reserve bottling, made exclusively for visitors.

10-Year-Old

Light and delicate, with notes of honey, nectarine, and banana cake and with a sweet creaminess throughout.

★ ABV: 40% ★ Type: Single Malt

16-Year-Old

Aged in a combination of ex-bourbon, port, and sherry casks, the resulting whiskey has big, fruity flavors balanced with vanilla and honey, wrapped in a soft, creamy mouthfeel.

★ ABV: 40% ★ Type: Single Malt

Bushmills 1608

First released in 2008 to celebrate 400 years since King James I granted the license to distill whiskey in Antrim. A superb whiskey with notes of citrus, cinnamon, and ginger cookies.

★ ABV: 46% ★ Type: Single Malt

James Joyce and whiskey

The Old Bushmills Distillery was officially registered in 1784, although it is rumored that distilling had been carried out on the site for over a century by then. As one of the oldest whiskeys in Ireland, Bushmills crops up regularly in the realms of music, motion pictures, and literature.

Bushmills is drunk by characters in movies including Sidney Lumet's courtroom drama *The Verdict*, the biopic *The Doors*, and more recently in *The Girl with the Dragon Tattoo*. Poet Seamus Heaney referenced the drink in his piece *The Bookcase*.

James Joyce's 1922 modernist masterpiece *Ulysses* also credits the whiskey. Molly Bloom, the wife of central character Leopold Bloom, mentions it in a rambling, unpunctuated section in the final chapter:

"... he never forgot himself when I was there sending me out of the room on some blind excuse paying his compliments the Bushmills whisky talking of course but hed do the same to the next woman that came along I suppose he died of galloping drink ages ago ... (sic)"

Joyce's father John had been a shareholder and the secretary in Dublin's Phoenix Park distillery. However, when it was closed in 1921, he was made bankrupt.

Ulysses is celebrated each year on "Bloomsday," which is held on June 16 in Dublin. Joyce fans dress in Edwardian costume, hold readings from the book and act out some of the events in it. They are even known to sip the odd whiskey.

Connemara

Connemara was first released in 1996 and was a totally fresh brand created by the team at the Cooley distillery in County Louth. Connemara is the only peated Irish whiskey available, and since its release it has been blowing away preconceptions about Irish whiskey. For years in Ireland only two distilleries were working, Midleton and Bushmills. Both made unpeated whiskeys and triple-distilled their spirit (they still do), which over time gave the impression to the whiskey drinkers of the world that this is how Irish whiskey always was. The truth is, however, that Ireland would have once had many peated styles of whiskey, just like Scotland. But due to the introduction of cheaper, more accessible fuels for drying malt and the tax implemented on malted barley, the peated style began to die out in Ireland, until eventually it was lost. Connemara changed all that, and over the years has helped attract many whiskey fans to take a fresh look at Irish whiskey.

With its whiskeys, Connemara, Tyrconnell, and the blend Kilbeggan, the Cooley distillery has become a cornerstone of the Irish whiskey movement since its founding in 1987. So much so that the distillery caught the eye of Beam Global (owner of Jim Beam, Laphroaig, and Canadian Club, to name but a few). In 2011 Beam bought Cooley for $95 million and with it Connemara and the other Cooley brands. The Connemara Peated range consists of the standard NAS (no age statement) bottling, a Cask Strength, a 12-year-old, and Turf Mor. A handful of single-cask and limited releases have been available, including an unusual release called Bog Oak, which was matured in 2,000-year-old oak found preserved in an Irish bog.

Connemara

A sweet, smoky nose with underlying flavors of green fruit and cotton candy, balanced with earthy peat and subtle vanilla.

✱ ABV: 40% ✱ Type: Single Malt

Connemara Cask Strength

An intense whiskey—brace yourself. Bonfire smoke and green herbaceous notes on the nose, with tarry peat and oak on the palate leading to a long, sweet, smoky finish.

✱ ABV: 57.9% ✱ Type: Single Malt

Green Spot

Green Spot whiskey was first created by Dublin-based spirit merchants Mitchells & Son. Casks of pure pot still whiskey were bought from the old Jameson distillery in Bow Street, and carefully matured and married together by the Mitchells to be sold in their shop. This practice was once very much the norm, with many distilleries selling casks to merchants who would then sell the spirit under a name of their choosing, but over time this has diminished in Ireland. Today the whiskey is still made for Mitchells & Son, but the production, blending, and bottling are carried out at the Midleton distillery. Finding Green Spot outside of Ireland can sometimes be tricky, but not impossible. Two whiskeys currently exist in the range: Green Spot and Yellow Spot, the latter being aged for 12 years.

Green Spot

Fresh, full, and spicy with ripe fruit and vanilla flavors combining with oaky spice and a grainy sweetness.

★ ABV: 40% ★ Type: Pure Pot Still

Kilbeggan

The Kilbeggan distillery in the town of Kilbeggan was founded in 1757 and is the oldest whiskey distillery in the world. Unlike Bushmills and Jameson, Kilbeggan didn't survive the Irish whiskey crisis and closed from 1957 until 2007, when once again spirit flowed. The rebirth of the distillery was spearheaded by the Cooley distillery, which in the years prior to restoration had reestablished the brand, making a blended whiskey under the Kilbeggan name. The distillery makes a number of spirit styles, including single malt whiskey and pure pot still whiskey (using a mix of malted and unmalted barley). The current Kilbeggan range consists of the standard bottling, an 18-year-old, and a single malt distillery reserve exclusive.

Kilbeggan

An easy-drinking and approachable blend with notes of lemon loaf cake, honey, vanilla, and subtle oaky spice.

★ ABV: 40% ★ Type: Blended Irish

WHAT THEY SAY ...

"The light music of whiskey falling into a glass— an agreeable interlude."

—James Joyce

Jameson

Jameson whiskey was first introduced in 1780, and was made by John Jameson at the Bow Street distillery in Dublin. John's commitment to quality all those years ago quickly helped to establish the whiskey as a key player in the industry, and by 1820 Jameson's had become Ireland's second largest distilling company. The distillery's fortunes rose and fell over the next century with the fluctuations of Irish whiskey, and in 1966 a bold move was undertaken by the four distilling companies that had weathered the bad times, namely to combine their resources by creating a large company called Irish Distillers.

In 1975 the new company built a brand new distillery at the site of the old Midleton distillery in County Cork, which was to become the new home of Jameson and a dozen other brands, bringing to an end nearly 200 years of distilling at the original site in Dublin. Today Jameson's enjoys enormous success, being the number-one selling Irish whiskey and sitting among the top 20 best-selling whiskeys in the world, with 48 million bottles sold globally in 2012.

Jameson

Light floral notes and pepper on the nose, with a soft sherry, vanilla, and sweet spiciness on the palate and finish.

✴ ABV: 40% ✴ TYPE: Blended Irish

12-Year-Old, Special Reserve

Richer and fuller than the standard bottling and incredibly easy-drinking with honey, vanilla, oak, and rich sherry flavors throughout.

✴ ABV: 40% ✴ TYPE: Blended Irish

Midleton

The new Midleton Distillery was built in 1975 in County Cork in order to consolidate the brands of Jameson and John Powers & Son, which had together formed the company Irish Distillers in 1966 in order to make production of their multiple brands more efficient. This was done in a bid to save what was at the time a collapsing industry. The distillery is a feat of engineering genius, and is capable of producing the multiple spirit styles needed to replicate the brands from the distilleries it replaced. The Midleton whiskey itself has long been the most premium Irish whiskey available and is only released once a year in limited quantities, hence the name, Midleton Very Rare. The occasional special release can be found.

Midleton Barry Crockett Legacy

A pure pot still expression of Midleton carrying the name of the master distiller. Notes of sweet pipe tobacco, honeycomb, toffee, and citrus.

★ ABV: 46% ★ TYPE: Pure Pot Still

Paddy

This popular Irish blend enjoys a cultlike status in some parts of the world, but on the whole is less known than many of its Irish cousins. The whiskey is said to take its name from a gregarious salesman called Patrick J. O'Flaherty, who worked for Cork Distilleries. Paddy, as he was otherwise known, was by all accounts a memorable fellow and was well known for standing a round of his favorite whiskey at the various establishments he visited. Over time he became so synonymous with the whiskey he was selling that when customers rang to place orders they would frequently ask for a case of Paddy's. This went on for years until in 1912 the company eventually adopted the name "Paddy" as a tribute to its best salesman; prior to this it had gone by the name Cork Distilleries Company Old Irish Whiskey.

Paddy

The nose is fresh, with a light floral note and a buttery sweetness. The palate is soft and creamy leading to a spicy, dry finish.

✶ ABV: 40% ✶ Type: Blended Irish

WHAT THEY SAY ...

"May the enemies of Ireland never eat bread nor drink whiskey, but be tormented with itching without benefit of scratching."

—Irish toast

Powers

Powers whiskey dates back to 1791, when James Power founded a distillery in John's Lane in Dublin. In 1809 the distillery became a limited company and began to grow at a substantial rate under the ownership of John Power. John was a shrewd businessman and a respected member of Dublin's community, receiving a baronetcy in 1841. The famous Gold Label brand, for which the whiskey is best known, was introduced in 1886, and is currently made at the Midleton distillery along with Jameson and several others. Powers is also credited with creating the world's first whiskey mini, called Baby Powers, which went on sale in 1920. The current range consists of the original Gold Label, 12-Year-Old Special Reserve, and a pure pot still release, Powers John's Lane.

Powers John's Lane

One of the best examples of the pure pot still style and highly recommended. Rich, with a weighty mouthfeel and notes of cocoa, toffee, leather, and dried stone fruit.

✶ ABV: 46% ✶ Type: Pure Pot Still

Tyrconnell

The Tyrconnell whiskey was originally made by the Watt family at their distillery in Derry. The brand takes its name from the famous racehorse "The Tyrconnell," which won the National Produce Stakes in Ireland in 1876 at odds of 100–1. The trusty steed just so happened to be owned by the Watts, and in commemoration the Tyrconnell brand was launched that same year. In its glory days the brand saw great success in the United States, being a big seller before Prohibition. But sadly during the great Irish whiskey decline of the 1920s, the Watt distillery closed, taking the Tyrconnell whiskey with it.

The brand remained in the graveyard of Irish whiskeys next to hundreds of others until 1988, when the Cooley distillery was built in County Louth. This marked a tipping point in the Irish whiskey industry, and helped to kick-start a much-needed revival. Upon its completion Cooley became the third whiskey distillery in Ireland and set about restoring the Tyrconnell brand. The whiskey is made using traditional pot stills and using 100 percent malted barley, making it one of very few Irish single malts. It's also only distilled twice, setting it apart from Bushmills and other well-known Irish brands. Since the rebirth of Tyrconnell the brand has scooped a number of awards and medals at spirit competitions the world over and is well on its way to being restored to its former glory. The core range consists of just the standard NAS bottling, but many releases have been made available over the years. These have included a number of ten-year-old wood-finished expressions from port, sherry, Madeira, and a handful of different wine casks.

Tyrconnell

Sweet and easy-drinking with a soft, creamy mouthfeel and subtle notes of citrus, honey, and vanilla.

★ ABV: 40% ★ TYPE: Single Malt

10-Year-Old Port Cask Finish

Thick, jammy fruit and notes of marmalade and oak combine with honey, vanilla, and sweet spice.

★ ABV: 46% ★ TYPE: Single Malt

Redbreast

Redbreast whiskey began life at the Jameson distillery in Dublin, and was first launched in 1939 as the brand name given to the pure pot still whiskey supplied by Jameson to other blenders and bottlers. Today the whiskey is made at the Midleton distillery and has become the flagship brand of the pure pot still style. This style of whiskey is unique to Ireland, in which both malted and unmalted barley are mixed together prior to distillation. It's widely accepted that this style came about as a way to avoid paying tax that was levied on malted barley. Redbreast whiskey has a huge following, which has beyond a doubt helped champion what nearly became a forgotten style of whiskey. The core Redbreast range consists of the 12-, 15- and 21-year-olds, as well as a cask-strength 12-year-old.

Redbreast 12-Year-Old

A rich, complex whiskey delivered in a soft, creamy style with notes of dried fruit and nuts alongside banana cake and oaky spice.

✹ ABV: 40% ✹ Type: Pure Pot Still

Tullamore DEW

Whiskey was first made in 1829 at the Tullamore distillery in County Offaly under the ownership of distiller Michael Molloy. In 1857 the distillery passed to his nephew, Bernard Daly, and in 1862 the young Daniel E. Williams started his working life at the distillery on the malting floor. Daniel worked his way up the ladder and in 1887 he became the general manager and later part-owner with the Daly family. Daniel is credited with creating the successful brand Tullamore DEW and for spearheading expansion of the distillery; in homage his initials became part of the brand name. The whiskey has been made at Midleton distillery since the 1970s, but in 2013 the new owners of the brand, William Grant & Sons, announced the rebuilding of the distillery in County Offaly.

Tullamore DEW

Green fruit and citrus notes on the nose, with soft oak, vanilla, and marzipan on the palate and finish.

✹ ABV: 40% ✹ Type: Blended Irish

WHAT THEY SAY ...

"I wouldn't be here if it wasn't for my mum. I know I've got Irish blood because I wake up everyday with a hangover."

—Noel Gallagher

NORTH AMERICA

As they celebrated the 80th anniversary of the end of Prohibition in 2013, American distillers toasted a rediscovered love of their national spirits.

Consumption in the United States of straight American whiskey, a category that includes bourbon, rye, corn whiskey, and Tennessee whiskey, grew by 5.2 percent in 2012, and it shows no sign of abating. Such is the renewed thirst for these drinks that some in the industry have reported future supply worries, as the market sector struggles to keep up with rampant demand.

There are several reasons contributing to the good news for American whiskeys. Some commentators point to the retro appeal of TV shows like *Mad Men*, where the characters happily knock back hard liquor, immune to current health concerns. Others point to the "straight" nature of bourbon and other whiskeys, in that they are very pure drinks with a sense of heritage and no additives, something that plays well in marketing terms.

Legally, American straight whiskey is distilled from a fermented cereal grain mash creating a spirit not exceeding 80 percent ABV. It is then aged for at least two years in oak barrels. Filtering and water dilution are the only permitted modifications for straight whiskey prior to its bottling.

The spirit has not always been made with this level of care. American whiskey started its life as a raw, unaged spirit, distilled to fortify the early colonists of the new frontier. It took many years before it developed into the distinctively American bourbons, ryes, and Tennessee whiskeys that are available today.

In fact, the earliest spirits drunk by settlers had to be imported from Europe. This was costly and time-consuming, and

Americans were soon trying to produce their own spirits. An early innovation was the use of rye instead of barley. European barley did not crop well on the new continent, whereas rye did, and over time the native corn was also introduced.

Until the mid-eighteenth century, whiskey was made in relatively small quantities, mainly by farmer-distillers. It was an ideal way of using up surplus grain, and the end result was certainly easier to transport. In rural communities, whiskey was used for barter.

Whiskey achieved a higher profile when President George Washington took a particular interest in the spirit. As well as

There was room for both drinks over the next century as the whiskey industry grew and became more sophisticated. However, this growth was paralleled by the surge of the Temperance Movement, which ultimately led to the banning of brewing and distilling in the United States from 1920 to 1933.

Except it didn't stop entirely. As well as massive illicit production and smuggling of whiskey, some distilleries carried on producing whiskey for "medicinal" purposes. The government issued ten licenses to produce medicinal whiskey, although

suggesting that public distilleries be constructed to service the needs of the army, he distilled his own rye whiskey, encouraged by his Scottish farm manager James Anderson.

In Kentucky, distillers were busily creating what some see as America's only native drink, bourbon. The first commercial distillery was opened in 1783 by Evan Williams, while Elijah Craig's decision to char corn whiskey is seen by some as a defining moment in the creation of bourbon.

Neighboring Tennessee went off on its own tack following the 1825 invention by Alfred Eaton of the Lincoln County Process. This filtration system sees the whiskey pass through a ten-foot-deep casing of maple charcoal and is held to account for the mellower flavor of whiskeys such as Jack Daniel's.

In Kentucky, distillers were busily creating what some see as America's only native drink, bourbon.

only six were ever activated—by Stitzel, Glenmore, Schenley, Brown-Forman, National Distilleries, and Frankfort Distilleries.

When Prohibition ended, the United States whiskey industry could start to recover. It had stiff competition, as Canadian and Scotch whisky had gained a valuable foothold, as had clear spirits such as gin. However, it has gradually made a comeback, with clever marketing and a focus on quality from such brands as Jack Daniel's, Maker's Mark, Jim Beam, and Wild Turkey. Having viewed America as a country that imported huge amounts of spirits, the world started to wake up to American brands.

The craft of American whiskey-making led one whiskey guru, Jim Murray, author of the best-selling *Jim Murray's Whisky Bible*, to proclaim that bourbon had overtaken Scotch, and that the best whiskey was

now coming from Kentucky, where Buffalo Trace was "arguably the best distillery in the world."

To the north of America, Canada's whisky (without an "e") is also undergoing something of a positive reappraisal. Its distinctive rye whisky often doesn't contain that much actual rye, as Canadian distillers have traditionally used it sparingly as a flavoring to provide spicy, floral, and sour qualities.

New small-batch brands are winning over critics, bartenders and whisky aficionados, much as special releases and craft distillers have helped reinvigorate the American spirit. And like their American cousins, the Canadians hope that drinkers are looking to trade up to higher-end brands that offer more prestige and better profits.

KENTUCKY

Kentucky is famously the home of bourbon whiskey, producing 95 percent of the world's supply. The drink doesn't have to be made there—many United States craft distilleries produce their own versions—but the big names such as Jim Beam, Maker's Mark, Wild Turkey, and Four Roses all hail from the bluegrass state.

As the saying goes, all bourbon is whiskey, but not all whiskey is bourbon. To qualify as straight bourbon, the drink has to be distilled in the United States from at least 51 percent corn, and aged in charred new oak barrels for at least two years. Only water may be added before bottling.

Bourbon production started in Virginia, before Kentucky became a separate state, in the 1700s. Corn cultivation in the area had been encouraged by Virginia's "corn patch and cabin rights," which granted free land to settlers who grew the crop. It was easy to cultivate and it also made a distinctive style of whiskey, lighter than the rye whiskey from the east. The spirit was also easier than grain to get to market.

Many of the brands associated with bourbon production today date from the late 1700s. Jacob Beam (Jim Beam) built his first distillery in 1788. Robert Samuels (Maker's Mark) arrived in 1780.

Kentucky is famously the home of bourbon whiskey, producing 95 percent of the world's supply.

Elijah Pepper (James E. Pepper and Old Crow) settled in Old Pepper Springs, Kentucky, in 1776.

The name "bourbon" refers to Bourbon County, which was stamped as the place of origin on barrels of spirit. Bourbon's place in U.S. history was officially recognized by Congress in 1964, when it was declared a distinctive product of the United States.

In recent years demand has soared, and production has risen more than 120 percent since 1999 to more than one million barrels in 2012, according to the Kentucky Distillers' Association.

A side effect of this is that most of the big producers have been bought up by foreign owners. Jim Beam and Maker's Mark were recently bought by Suntory. Four Roses is owned by Kirin and Wild Turkey by Campari.

Although bourbon reigns supreme in Kentucky, the state also produces some rye whiskeys such as Sazerac Rye, produced by Buffalo Trace, and Knob Creek Straight Rye. Just don't try making a mint julep with them.

Blanton's

Blanton's was the first single-barrel bourbon to be released and was championed by Elmer T. Lee, who was manager at Buffalo Trace for many years until he retired in 1985. Unlike most bourbons, for which many casks are married together to create a consistent flavor profile, with a single barrel release only one cask, of exceptional quality and character, will be bottled. The whiskey takes its name from Colonel Albert B. Blanton, who in his 55 years of working at the distillery would select the occasional cask to bottle for family and a select few who were in his favor. Blanton's was first launched in 1984, and since then has established itself as one of the greats, undoubtedly also raising the benchmark for bourbon in general.

Special Reserve

Spiced sweet fruit, buttery pastry and caramel on the nose, with chocolate orange and toffee on the palate and finish.

✳ ABV: 40% ✳ TYPE: Bourbon

Buffalo Trace

The Buffalo Trace distillery is home to many of the well-known bourbons that can be found across the world today. The distillery is named after the buffalo trails that were formed by enormous herds of migrating buffalo. These "traces" were followed by settlers to help them find fertile land, and to begin their new lives in what was then an inhospitable and unknown world. Distilling is said to have been carried out on the site in these early settlements, but the distillery that stands today wasn't built until 1857. Buffalo Trace is regarded as one of the oldest distilleries in the United States, and has been the home to many of the bourbon industry's pioneers. The Buffalo Trace brand was launched in 1999, when the distillery was rechristened and renamed Buffalo Trace; before that it had been known as George T. Stagg.

Buffalo Trace

Spicy and sweet on the nose, with candy apples and vanilla toffee on the palate, leading to a sweet, spicy finish.

✳ ABV: 40% ✳ TYPE: Bourbon

Bulleit

The Bulleit bourbon was first created in the 1830s by a Louisville tavern owner called Augustus Bulleit. Augustus had tried many different mash bills in his quest for a unique style of bourbon and finally settled on a recipe with a much higher percentage of rye. After establishing a successful business, Augustus mysteriously vanished, taking his bourbon along with him. The reasons for his disappearance remain a mystery to this day. It wasn't until 1987 that the whiskey was revived by Tom Bulleit, great-great-grandson of Augustus. Tom left his job in a successful law firm to pursue his goal of restoring the brand to its former glory. The whiskey is made using the original recipe and is now available all over the world. The range includes the Bulleit bourbon, a rye, and a 10-year-old.

Bulleit Bourbon

Toffee and oaky spice on the nose, with a cinnamon and cider, doughnut flavor on the palate and vanilla on the finish.

✵ ABV: 45% ✵ Type: Bourbon

Eagle Rare

Eagle Rare is a renowned single-barrel bourbon that is widely available and held in high regard. The brand was acquired by Buffalo Trace in the late 1980s, prior to which it was owned by Seagram, who had created the bourbon in 1975. Its modern single-barrel form was first released as a 17-year-old in 2000 as part of the Antique Collection from Buffalo Trace. The 10-year-old was introduced a few years later and is one of the best-priced single-barrel bourbons available. Eagle Rare uses the same mash bill as the Buffalo Trace brand, but is left to mature in what the Trace team regard as a superior part of the warehousing for maturation. The subtle differences found in various areas of Trace's warehousing, over time, encourage different flavors to emerge.

WHAT THEY SAY ...

"Happiness is having a rare steak, a bottle of whiskey, and a dog to eat the rare steak."

—Johnny Carson

Single Barrel 10-Year-Old

Toffee, honey, and herbs on the nose, with cocoa and almonds on the palate leading to a dry, spicy finish.

✵ ABV: 45% ✵ Type: Bourbon

Elijah Craig

In bourbon lore it is said that the Reverend Elijah Craig came up with the idea of using the charred cask, which has become standard practice among bourbon producers. The story goes that, during a fire at the reverend's distillery at some point in the 1780s, a number of oak casks were caught in the blaze and became heavily charred. Nonetheless, Elijah used the casks, and noticed that when the spirit was later drawn off, the whiskey had improved dramatically. As with most tales surrounding brands, this one is best taken with a pinch of salt. However, Heaven Hill named its whiskey in honor of Elijah Craig, Baptist minister and distiller.

12-Year-Old

Toasty oak and a creamy sweetness on the nose; the palate is soft and mellow, with stewed fruit and spices and hints of aniseed in the finish.

✳ ABV: 47% ✳ TYPE: Bourbon

Evan Williams

Evan Williams is currently the second-best-selling bourbon in the United States and is a well-known brand, both domestically and around the globe. The whiskey takes its name from Evan Williams, an emigrant of Welsh origin, who traveled to the frontier in the 1700s. Evan was considered a jack-of-all-trades, being among other things a farmer, building contractor, politician, and, of course, a distiller. Evan first distilled whiskey in Kentucky in 1783 and is believed by some to be Kentucky's first distiller. The whiskey is made at Heaven Hill's Bernheim distillery in Louisville, which it bought from Diageo in 1999. There are a handful of expressions available; these include the Black, Green, and White labels, a small-batch release called 1783, and a selection of vintage/single-barrel releases.

Black Label

Oaky cola and vanilla on the nose, with cherry syrup and cinnamon toast on the palate and a decent firm finish.

✳ ABV: 43% ✳ TYPE: Bourbon

Four Roses

The origin of the Four Roses name is shrouded in mystery and has many different versions. The popular story peddled today is that it was inspired by a marriage proposal made by distillery founder Paul Jones Jr. His young lady informed him that her answer would be "Yes" if she arrived at the forthcoming grand ball wearing four roses as her corsage. Lo and behold, at the ball she was wearing four roses, and as a symbol of his love Paul named his whiskey Four Roses. The brand had originally been a blended bourbon that was sold in the United States before the distillery was bought by Seagram in 1941. Four Roses is one of the best-selling bourbons worldwide, especially in Europe and Asia. The range today consists of Yellow, Small Batch, Single Barrel, Platinum, and Fine Old.

Small Batch

A gutsy, full-bodied bourbon with bags of character and notes of caramel, vanilla, and red berries.

★ ABV: 45% ★ Type: Bourbon

George T. Stagg

Like many whiskeys from the Trace stable, George T. Stagg bears the name of one of the distillery's historical figures. George began working with the distillery almost 150 years ago and, together with E. H. Taylor Jr., he helped shape the distillery into the success it is today. George was so influential that the distillery was rechristened to bear his name for a number of decades from 1904. It seems fitting that such an important figure in the distillery's history should be immortalized in what is the most premium bourbon available today. The George T. Stagg whiskey was introduced with the third release of the Antique Collection in the autumn of 2002. Each year has seen a new release of Stagg, all of which have been bottled from only a handful of casks, at barrel proof (aka cask strength) and with no filtration.

Bourbon, 2013 Release

An incredibly rich whiskey with intense oaky and chocolate notes, a weighty mouthfeel, and a vast array of flavor.

★ ABV: 64.1% ★ Type: Bourbon

WHAT THEY SAY ...

"I should never have switched from Scotch to Martinis."

—Humphrey Bogart's last words

Georgia Moon

In other whiskey-making countries Georgia Moon wouldn't technically qualify as whiskey, as no minimum aging has been observed, which would in theory put it in line with other unaged spirits like vodka. It is an unusual quirk of the American whiskey industry that it allows new-make spirit to qualify as whiskey. Unaged new-make whiskey has been sold under many names over the years, such as White Dog, White Lightning, and Moonshine. When spirit like this was sold—for example during Prohibition—it would most likely have been at full, off-the-still strength, in many cases flavored with fruit to tamp down the aggressive young spirit. This style of whiskey is enjoying a small revival across the United States, with many different flavored varieties coming to market from new startup distilleries.

Georgia Moon

A clean nose with a trace of buttery corn. The immaturity of the spirit becomes apparent on the palate, nevertheless an interesting whiskey.

★ ABV: 40% ★ Type: Corn

Heaven Hill

Heaven Hill was built in 1935, two years after the end of Prohibition, by the Shapira family, who still own and operate the business, making Heaven Hill the largest family-owned distiller in the United States. Like Buffalo Trace, the distillery makes many different brands under one roof, using different mash bills and techniques to create a wide spectrum of flavors. The distillery has always focused on bourbon but in more recent years has created an enormous portfolio of other spirits, too. In 1996 a devastating fire destroyed much of the maturing stock and nearly crippled the company. Production today takes place at the Bernheim distillery, while the Heaven Hill facility in Bardstown is used for maturation and bottling. Heaven Hill Bourbon, Elijah Craig, Evan Williams, and Fighting Cock are just a few of the whiskeys produced by Heaven Hill.

Heaven Hill

The flagship bourbon from Heaven Hill and aged for four years, this is a straightforward bourbon normally used in cocktails.

★ ABV: 40% ★ Type: Bourbon

"How well I remember my first encounter with The Devil's Brew. I happened to stumble across a case of bourbon —and went right on stumbling for several days thereafter."

—W.C. Fields

Jim Beam

The Beam family originated from Germany, emigrating to the United States in the mid-1700s, and Jacob Beam was the first member of the family to make whiskey in Kentucky. Jacob's original distillery was called Old Tub and produced its first whiskey in 1795, by the name of Old Jake Beam. The brand as we know it today takes its name from James Beam, Jacob's great-grandson, who rebuilt the distillery in Clermont shortly after Prohibition ended in 1933. The making of Jim Beam whiskey is still in the hands of the family, with Frederick Noe, great-grandson of James, being the master distiller today. The current range from Jim Beam is extensive, but the main bottlings for which the distillery is best known are the classic White/Black labels and more recently Devil's Cut.

Devil's Cut

Richer and fuller than other Jim Beam expressions with a bit more kick, plenty of vanilla, and woody spice.

★ ABV: 45%
★ Type: Bourbon

Knob Creek

Knob Creek first arrived in the early 1990s along with two other brands from the Jim Beam stable, Bakers seven-year-old and Basil Hayden's. All three were additions to Booker Noe's (sixth generation of the Beam Family) Small Batch selection, which appeared in 1988. The concept behind Knob Creek was a return to pre-Prohibition-style bourbon, aged for longer and bottled at a higher ABV. The brand quickly established itself as a player in what was then a very small premium bourbon category. With its higher rye content in the mash, higher strength, age of nine years and overall more heavyweight character, it soon became a hit. Since its release, a handful of other Knob Creek bottlings have emerged including a Single Barrel, Rye, and Smoked Maple expression.

Knob Creek Nine-Year-Old

Caramel and white chocolate on the nose, with tingling oaky spice and vanilla on the palate leading to a long, woody finish.

★ ABV: 50%
★ Type: Bourbon

Larceny

Part of the Old Fitzgerald family of whiskeys, acquired by Heaven Hill in 1999. The brand takes its name from the crooked treasury agent, John E. Fitzgerald. In the late 1800s treasury agents were the only men legally allowed to carry the keys to the vast warehouses of maturing stock being produced by Kentucky's distillers. John, as it happens, had quite a taste for good bourbon and is said to have dipped into plenty of barrels—so much so that the whiskeys he selected began to make a name for themselves. Larceny is a wheated bourbon, where the rye in the mash bill has been replaced with wheat, making for a softer, more easy-drinking style. Only 100 casks between six and 12 years old are selected to make each batch of Larceny.

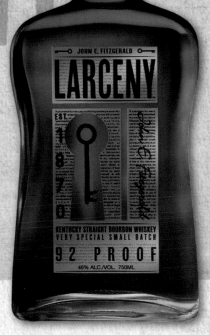

Larceny

Brown sugar, honey, and cinnamon on the nose with a soft, creamy palate and a long, spicy finish.

★ ABV: 46%
★ Type: Bourbon

Maker's Mark

Of all the bourbons, Maker's Mark is probably the easiest to spot behind a bar, and its iconic red wax seal and square bottle have almost certainly helped propel the brand to success. The whiskey is made by the Samuels family, who can trace their distilling heritage back to the late 1700s. Currently the distillery has Bill Samuels Jr. at the helm, with his son Rob (the eighth generation of Samuels) waiting in the wings. The whiskey famously came about when Bill Samuels Sr. deliberately burned the original 170-year-old family recipe in his determined pursuit of a superior and better-quality spirit than that of his forebears. Needless to say the gamble paid off, and since the first release of Maker's Mark in 1958 the brand has gone from strength to strength. Maker's Mark has two main expressions: namely the 45 percent standard bottling and the newer 46 percent release.

Maker's Mark

Notes of honey and exotic fruit on the nose, with vanilla and nutty flavors on the palate leading to a warming spicy finish.

★ ABV: 45% ★ Type: Bourbon

Mellow Corn

Corn whiskey has been a forgotten spirit for many decades, but in the last few years signs of a revival have been seen, with a handful of craft distillers seizing on its uniqueness as a selling point. Corn whiskey was a popular illicit spirit during Prohibition, since corn was abundant and also cheap. This illicit corn whiskey was often sold in jars and would have been sold straight off the still as new make or White Dog. Corn whiskey has two main differences from bourbon, the first being the mash bill. In bourbon a minimum of 51 percent corn must be used, whereas in corn whiskey the minimum must be 81 percent. The second difference is that corn whiskey can be aged in second-fill casks, whereas bourbon must by law use virgin oak casks. This release is part of the Heaven Hill family.

Mellow Corn

Vanilla, banana, and honey on the nose, with ginger and more vanilla on the palate; the finish is short and sweet.

★ ABV: 50% ★ Type: Corn

Noah's Mill

The Noah's Mill brand is relatively modern compared to its competitors and is made by the Kentucky Bourbon Distillers Co. (KBDC), also known as the Willett Distillery Co. The KBDC is run by the descendants of the Willett family, who were distillers in Kentucky from the 1800s and operated their own family distillery from the 1930s through to the 1980s. The company then ceased trading until a few years later, when it was purchased and renamed Kentucky Bourbon Distillers Ltd. Thanks to the current generation of the Willett family, the company has bounced back, the original distillery has been restored, and once again whiskey is being made. The company is now the owner of seven successful brands, which are available in many countries, namely Old Bardstown, Johnny Drum, Willett Kentucky Vintage, Pure Kentucky XO, Noah's Mill, and Rowan's Creek.

Noah's Mill

Toffee, coffee, and woody spice on the nose, dark fruit on the palate, and a strong finish with charred oak and plenty of grip.

★ ABV: 57.15% ★ Type: Bourbon

Rittenhouse

Rittenhouse Rye belongs to the Heaven Hill family and has become hugely popular in the last few years, as rye whiskey begins to grow in popularity. The global demand for rye whiskey has increased enormously as pre-Prohibition-style popular culture has become fashionable. Rye whiskey is the key ingredient in a good Manhattan cocktail, and as a result many bartenders require at least one solid and consistent rye whiskey for the back bar. This is where Rittenhouse has excelled: being a good price and benefiting from Heaven Hill's distribution network, the brand has become a favorite of bartenders the world over. The Rittenhouse range consists of the standard Straight Rye and 100 proof. There have also been a handful of limited releases, including a single-barrel 25-year-old.

Rittenhouse Rye 100 Proof

A lively nose, with cocoa and a rye spiciness. The palate is intensely oaky and full-bodied leading to a long, spicy finish.

✴ ABV: 50%
✴ Type: Rye

Pappy Van Winkle— small is beautiful

Most companies increase production as demand for their product grows, hopefully gaining a larger share of the market in the process.

However, one bourbon company has flipped that logic on its head and limited production to just 7,000 cases a year. By comparison Jim Beam sells around seven million cases a year. But this process of planned restriction of supply has turned Pappy Van Winkle into one of the world's most coveted spirits. Drinkers are known to submit themselves to waiting lists of ten years or more in order to get hold of a single bottle. They retail for around $200, but sell for ten times that in secondary markets.

It wasn't always the case. The brand dates back to 1893, when Julian "Pappy" Van Winkle, who adorns the label, started working as a liquor salesman. He graduated to owning the Stitzel-Weller distillery, which produced bourbon until being closed in 1991.

By that time the Van Winkles had sold the business and bourbon demand was declining. However, Van Winkle's grandson, Julian, bought up supplies of the aged bourbon and continued to sell it. In 2002 production was handed to Buffalo Trace distillery, which has produced the liquor since then.

The scarcity of Pappy Van Winkle was highlighted when the theft of several hundred bottles from the bonded warehouse made international news in 2013. Police offered a $10,000 reward for information, but to no avail. The culprits were not found.

Sazerac

Sazerac Rye whiskey takes its name from a famous cocktail produced in the Sazerac Coffee House in Exchange Alley, New Orleans, in the 1850s. The cocktail was originally made using a cognac called Sazerac de Forges et Fils, but in the late 1800s the cocktail evolved and began to use rye whiskey that originated from the Buffalo Trace distillery. This was partly due to the devastation of France's vineyards by the parasite *Phylloxera vastatrix*, which dealt a significant blow to cognac and wine production during this era, making cognac difficult to find and very expensive. The Sazerac Rye Whiskey from Buffalo Trace was first released in 2000 as part of their Antique Collection as an 18-year-old, but was introduced in its distinctive bottle as a regular release in 2005. Both expressions have received high acclaim in spirit competitions the world over.

Straight Rye

Chocolate orange and ginger on the nose with rich spicy fruit on the palate, finishing off with sweet spicy oak and vanilla.

★ ABV: 45% ★ Type: Rye

W. L. Weller

Like many bourbons, W. L. Weller takes its name from a significant historical figure in American whiskey production. In the late 1800s, William Larue Weller became the first in the industry to create a bourbon with a high wheat content. The high proportion of wheat used in the mash bill made for a lighter, softer, and generally more approachable spirit than its heavier rye-based cousins and soon became a big success. Sadly the distillery where this whiskey was originally made was closed in 1992, but fortunately the brand lives on at the Buffalo Trace distillery, after they acquired it in 1999. There are currently three expressions of W. L. Weller available: the Special Reserve, Antique, and a 12-year-old.

12-Year-Old

A lighter, more easygoing bourbon with notes of toffee and butterscotch wrapped in soft, woody spice.

★ ABV: 40% ★ Type: Bourbon

Wild Turkey

The Wild Turkey distillery, as it is now known, was first built in the 1850s and was originally known as Old Moore. In 1869 the distillery was bought by the Ripy family, who at the time had interests in many distilleries, and were major suppliers of bourbon to merchants, blenders, and bottlers. Wild Turkey did not acquire its iconic name until much later in the 1940s, by which time the distillery had changed names and ownership a few times. The brand is hugely well-known today and is made by one of the industry's oldest figures, Jimmy Russell, who has worked at the distillery since 1954. As with many well-established brands, the Wild Turkey range is extensive; the core bottlings consist of the 81 proof, 101 proof, an eight-year-old 101 proof, and the Rare Breed expression.

Wild Turkey 101

A gutsy, full-bodied bourbon with plenty of clout, notes of butterscotch, vanilla, and a big, spicy kick.

★ ABV: 50.5% ★ Type: Bourbon

Woodford Reserve

The Woodford distillery is officially the oldest standing bourbon distillery in Kentucky, with distillation beginning in 1812 and continuing to this day. In 1833 the distillery took on a young Scottish scientist and master distiller called Dr. James Crow, who grew to be one of the most important figures in the history of American distilling. During his 20 years at Woodford, Crow perfected many methods of production, like the sour mash. He is often (and rightly) referred to as the "Father of Bourbon," as the detailed records he kept shaped and defined what we now know as the "straight whiskey." Woodford is unique among its competitors as it operates traditional pot stills, originating from Scotland. Alongside the core range the distillery continues to evolve, releasing a plethora of interesting releases, including some single malts in the Master's Collection.

Woodford Reserve

A complex, spicy bourbon with notes of honey, butterscotch, vanilla ice cream, and a trace of smoke.

★ ABV: 43.2% ★ Type: Bourbon

TENNESSEE

Historically, making whiskey was a well-practiced pursuit in Tennessee. By 1799 there were 61 stills recorded in Davidson County alone, serving a population of just 4,000. Today there are only about four producers, although one—Jack Daniel's —is among the biggest spirits brands in the world.

While most drinkers would describe Jack Daniel's as bourbon, that's not what it's called on the bottle. Jack Daniel's, Collier and McKeel, and George Dickel are the three best-known brands of Tennessee whiskey (or whisky, as George Dickel spells it). It is a type of bourbon, but is legally required to be "a straight Bourbon Whiskey authorized to be produced only in the State of Tennessee," according to the North American Free Trade Agreement (NAFTA).

As of May 2013, it is also required that Tennessee whiskeys are made using the Lincoln County Process. This is an additional stage during which the whiskey is filtered through, or steeped in, a layer of maple charcoal before it is barreled.

Proponents of the process claim it mellows the whiskey, allowing vanilla, caramel, and licorice flavors to emerge. Ironically, following the alteration of county boundaries, the only Tennessee whiskey that is still actually made in Lincoln County, Benjamin Prichard's, does not follow the process as it has a legal exemption.

Historically, making whiskey was a well-practiced pursuit in Tennessee.

Until 2009, only three of the 95 counties in Tennessee permitted distilling. However, following legal changes, 44 counties allow distilling, and small artisan brands of whiskey are starting to emerge, such as Nashville's Corsair Artisan, Peg Leg Porker bourbon, and Cumberland Cask.

These are producing on a small scale for whiskey connoisseurs and will have to go some way before they threaten the Moore County giant. Jack Daniel's sold 11 million cases of the classic Black Label in 2012–13 and is investing $100 million to boost production further. However, drinkers can only sample the spirit on the distillery tour as Tennessee is a dry county.

Corsair Artisan Distillery

The Corsair distillery in Nashville, Tennessee, was built in 2010 by distilling duo Andrew Webber and Darek Bell. Before working with whiskey both Andrew and Darek had focused on building a biodiesel plant, but after hitting a snag they decided their efforts would be better spent distilling spirits and making whiskey. Most craft distillers have some unusual quirks in their production and their products, but few have more than Corsair.

Corsair's distillery is split in two, with production taking place at two separate facilities. Fermentation and the first round of distillation take place at the newer facility in Nashville, whereas the final distillation and maturation take place at the original site at Bowling Green in Kentucky, where Corsair started in 2008. A whole host of experimental whiskeys have been released by Corsair, some of which have pushed the boundaries of American whiskey to the extreme. Their weird and wonderful range of spirits is ever-growing, and has seen no fewer than 22 releases, which have scooped up 41 medals from various spirit competitions.

The whiskeys in the range currently consist of Triple Smoke (a malt whiskey made using three different types of smoked malt), Wry Moon (unaged 100 percent rye whiskey), Ryemageddon (an aged version of Wry Moon), Grainiac (a nine-grain bourbon), Insane In The Grain (a 12-grain bourbon), Amarillo (a hopped bourbon), Rasputin (a hopped malt whiskey), and finally Quinoa Whiskey (made using malted barley and quinoa, a grain grown in South America). Aside from these various whiskeys a collection of other spirits can be found including rum, gin, and absinthe.

Ryemageddon

With a mash bill containing 80 percent rye supplemented with chocolate malt, red wheat, and malted rye, this is a truly unusual and powerful whiskey. Chocolaty, spicy, and chewy.

★ ABV: 46% ★ Type: Rye

Triple Smoke

Made with three types of malted barley dried using peat, cherry wood, and beech wood. The resulting whiskey is rich, smoky, and complex.

★ ABV: 40%
★ Type: Single Malt

George A. Dickel and Cascade Hollow

The George A. Dickel distillery is the other major distillery in Tennessee and operates in the shadow of the more famous Jack Daniel's. It takes its name from a spirits merchant from Nashville, who, like many other merchants of the time, would have bought and sold whiskey from multiple distilleries and vendors. Over time George narrowed his list of suppliers and purchased exclusive rights to sell from just the one distillery, which was then known as the Cascade Hollow distillery. The whiskey at this point was being sold under the name of George A. Dickel's Cascade Whisky. A few years later, in 1888, George's business partner and brother-in-law, Victor Shawb, acquired half the ownership of the Cascade distillery, followed by the other half around ten years later.

Contrary to popular belief and marketing spin, there is actually no real proof that George founded the Cascade Hollow distillery, although this is very much the official line peddled today. Come 1911 the whiskey industry in Tennessee took a turn for the worse as the state embraced the Temperance Movement, championing Prohibition nearly a decade before the rest of the United States. As a result the production and consumption of alcohol was outlawed and the distillery closed.

The company survived for a number of years, producing whiskey at a handful of different distilleries in Kentucky, and not returning home to Tennessee until 1958, when the distillery was rebuilt adjacent to the original site and accessing the same Cascade water source. The whiskey, like Jack Daniel's, uses the Lincoln County Process, filtering the spirit through charcoal prior to maturation. The Dickel range consists of No. 8, No. 12, Rye, and Barrel Select. An unusual quirk of George A. Dickel is that they spell "whisky" without an "e."

WHAT THEY SAY ...

"Truth is used to vitalize a statement rather than devitalize it. Truth implies more than a simple statement of fact. 'I don't have any whiskey,' may be a fact but it is not a truth."

—William S. Burroughs

No.12

A soft and sweet style with notes of dried fruit, oaky spice, popcorn, and a trace of sweet maple smoke.

★ ABV: 45%
★ TYPE: Blended

Rye

Made with a rye content of 95 percent and aged for at least five years, this whiskey is big, bold, and massively spicy.

★ ABV: 45%
★ TYPE: Rye

JACK DANIEL DISTILLERY
Lem Motlow, Prop., Inc.
DSP Tennessee - 1
Distiller

Old No.7

An uncomplicated whiskey and ideal for mixing. Notes of caramel, vanilla, banana toffee, and subtle, smoky char combine in a clean crisp character.

★ ABV: 40%

Single Barrel

Softer and more refined than the Old No. 7, offering a far greater depth of flavor, a better mouthfeel, and a longer finish.

★ ABV: 40%

Jack Daniel's

Of all the American whiskey brands, Jack Daniel's is probably the best known. Almost every bar in the world carries a bottle of Jack behind the bar, and between the clever advertising and legions of fans wearing various items of memorabilia, it's fairly safe to say that at some point almost every person has seen, or at least heard of, Jack Daniel's. No other whiskey in the world has managed to establish this cultlike status on such a huge scale, making the Jack Daniel's brand fall in line with other iconic brands such as Coca-Cola.

The distillery resides in Lynchburg, Tennessee, and although no one knows exactly when it was founded, it is generally accepted that it was at some point between 1860–80.

Jack Daniel's generally suffers from two major misconceptions, the first being that it is a bourbon. Production at Jack Daniel's mirrors bourbon production almost exactly, except for the use of the Lincoln County Process, which makes it a Tennessee whiskey. Only two distilleries in Tennessee employ this technique, and it distinguishes the whiskey from bourbon, where the process is not allowed.

The second common fallacy is that Jack Daniel's is not whiskey—this misunderstanding is usually only in the minds of the uneducated whiskey drinking public, who are unaware that whiskey is simply a mash of cereals and grains, fermented and then distilled. Over the years many limited expressions of Jack Daniel's have been made available, but the core whiskeys include the Old No. 7, Gentleman Jack, and the Single Barrel.

REST OF THE UNITED STATES

As well as the heartlands of distilling such as Tennessee and Kentucky, there were distilleries all over the United States before Prohibition. The www.pre-pro.com Distillery Database has tracked down 2,887 individual distilleries that were in operation prior to 1920.

Many folded in the 13 dry years leading up to the end of Prohibition in 1933, but in recent times there has been something of a rebirth in distilling, as whiskey makers have taken inspiration from the success of United States craft brewers and started to make small-batch whiskeys that are gaining a growing reputation.

According to an industry analysis presented at the American Distilling Institute (ADI) 2012 Conference, roughly 50 microdistilleries were operating in 2005. That number had grown to around 250 across 45 states by the time of the conference, and there are predictions that it could be as many as 1,000 in ten years' time. Many of them are on a microscale, encouraged by changes to state legislation that distinguish between megadistilleries and new start-ups in the size of the license fee. Prior to the change in the early 2000s it was too expensive for new entrants.

It takes time to develop a whiskey business, because the product needs to age and mature, but some of the

There were distilleries all over the United States before Prohibition.

new players are already attracting attention. In 2010, Scotch whisky giant William Grant & Sons bought the Hudson line of whiskeys, including a bourbon, a rye, and a malt, from New York-based Tuthilltown Spirits.

Many of the new players are steering clear of bourbon and trying their hand with other styles of American whiskey. There are a growing number to choose from: Stranahan's Colorado Whiskey is

a malt; Wasmund's produces single malt and rye whiskey; and Rock Town produces wheat whiskeys, including a hickory-smoked version.

New categories, such as that of very young white whiskey, are emerging, with producers such as Few Spirits, Buffalo Trace, and Low Gap paying homage to the age of moonshine.

Devil's Share

The Devil's Share whiskeys can be found in a portfolio of spirits from Ballast Point brewing and distilling. The company was set up by two home brewers, Jack White and Yuseff Cherney, and began in 1992 as a humble home-brewing store. Being enthusiasts and keen brewers it didn't take long for Jack and Yuseff to start making beer on a larger scale, and in 1996 they set up a backroom brewery behind the store. Demand for their beer continued to grow, and in 2004 the brewery moved to a larger facility called Scripps Ranch. By 2008 the pair were ready for another challenge and set up a distillery, thus becoming the first craft distillers in San Diego. Both the Devil's Share Single Malt and Bourbon were released in 2013.

Devil's Share Single Malt

Incredibly rich and sweet with plenty of vanilla, caramel, gummy fruit candies, and licorice.

★ ABV: 46% ★ TYPE: Single Malt ★ REGION: San Diego

Dry Fly

The Dry Fly distillery can be found in Spokane in Washington. On its completion in 2007 it became the first grain distillery in Washington in over 100 years. The name originates from the distillery's conception, since it was on a fly-fishing trip that owners Kent Fleischmann and Don Poffenroth decided to build a distillery. Like many new distilleries the Dry Fly team turned their immediate attention to producing vodka and gin, while laying down their whiskey to mature. Dry Fly has produced a number of interesting releases, and like many craft distillers it defies convention. Expressions so far have included Washington Wheat, Bourbon 101, Triticale (using a hybrid of wheat and rye grain), Port Finish Wheat Whiskey, and Peated Wheat Whiskey. The first Dry Fly single malt is currently maturing and is expected to arrive as a ten-year-old in 2017-18.

Washington Wheat

Soft and delicate, with notes of sweet pastry, oaky spice, coconut, and vanilla ice cream.

★ ABV: 40% ★ TYPE: Wheat ★ REGION: Washington

FEW

FEW is a craft distillery hailing from the city of Evanston, Chicago, an unlikely place for a distillery as Evanston is the home of Prohibition, born out of the Temperance Movement, which had a strong foothold in the city. The Temperance Movement was so well rooted in Evanston that anti-drinking laws far outlived the end of Prohibition in the 1930s, and drinking only became legal in the 1990s. Like many craft distillers FEW believes in a true grain-to-glass spirit, making sure that every drop of spirit sold under its label has run off its stills, and that all its ingredients are sourced locally. The range currently consists of a small-batch bourbon and a rye whiskey.

FEW Bourbon

A lively young bourbon, sweet and fruity, with toffee, marmalade, and oaky spice.

★ ABV: 46.5%
★ TYPE: Bourbon
★ REGION: Chicago

High West

The High West distillery began in 2004, led by whiskey enthusiast and biochemist David Perkins, and is the first distillery in Utah since the late 1800s. The team at High West are little known as whiskey specialists, but their various blends have collected some prestigious awards, and have created quite a buzz among enthusiasts. As with many start-up distilleries the initial problem faced after investment in equipment and casks is generating income while waiting for your maturing whiskey to come of age. This can be resolved by buying stock from other, older distilleries and blending casks to create a unique style, a technique practised throughout the centuries both in Scottish and American whiskey traditions. The High West team clearly have the ability to pick some great casks, bringing them together to create some interesting and unusual whiskeys.

Double Rye

Notes of mint and rye spice on the nose, with bold spice and vanilla on the palate and a sweet, spicy finish.

★ ABV: 46% ★ TYPE: Rye ★ REGION: Utah

WHAT THEY SAY ...

"Too much of anything is bad, but too much of good whiskey is barely enough."

——Mark Twain

Hudson

The Tuthilltown distillery in New York was created in 2003 and distilled the first grain spirit in New York in over 70 years. The project was set up by Ralph Erenzo with cofounder Brian Lee. The old mill from which the distillery was converted was originally bought by Ralph with the hope of turning it into a ranch for the many climbers who visited the area, but after a string of neighbor complaints, the project came to a halt.

At this point, they changed course and set about building a distillery. Like many craft outfits Hudson has a number of quirks in production, most notably the use of bass speakers in the barrel room. After receiving advice that they should shake their casks from time to time—a technique not without merit—the team came up with a simpler solution: bass speakers.

The heavy bass from the speakers agitates the casks and the maturing spirit, which Erenzo and Lee believe increases the spirit interaction with the oak and thus improves maturation. The experimentation with different grain recipes means that the Hudson range covers almost all U.S. whiskey styles: corn, rye, bourbon, single malt, and also a unique four grains bottling. Maturation takes place in casks of two different sizes, namely 3 gallons (13 liters) and 14 gallons (64 liters), made of American oak. Every whiskey is made using a small-batch process with spirit from a combination of the different barrel sizes. Since the project began, Hudson whiskey has been at the forefront of the craft distilling movement and has received a huge number of awards from major spirit competitions around the globe.

SON
k Corn
SKEY

HUDSON
SINGLE MALT
WHISKEY

375 ml   46% alc/vol
Made with 100% Malted Barley
Aged Under 4 Years in Oak
Hand Crafted and Bottled by:
Tuthilltown Spirits, Gardiner, New York

HUDSON
FOUR GRAIN BOURBON
WHISKEY

375 ml   46% alc/vol
Pot-Distilled From Corn, Rye, Wheat & Barley
Aged Under Four Years In Oak
Hand Crafted And Bottled By:
Tuthilltown Spirits, Gardiner, New York

Baby Bourbon

A sprightly young bourbon
that's soft and easygoing with
notes of vanilla, caramel, and
a subtle smokiness.

✶ ABV: 46% ✶ TYPE: Bourbon
✶ REGION: New York

New York Corn

An unaged spirit made with 100
percent corn. Sweet and buttery
with a creamy mouthfeel and
clean finish.

✶ ABV: 46% ✶ TYPE: Corn
✶ REGION: New York

HUDSON
BABY BOURBON
WHISKEY

375 ml   46% alc/vol
Made with 100% New York Corn
Aged under 4 yrs in American Oak
Handmade and Bottled by:
Tuthilltown Spirits, Gardiner, New York

HUDSON
New York Corn
WHISKEY

375 ml   46% alc/vol
Made with 100%
New York State Corn
Hand Crafted and Bottled by:
Tuthilltown Spirits, Gardiner, New York

Rock Town

Rock Town distillery is in the town of Little Rock in the State of Arkansas and is the first whiskey distillery to be established in the area since Prohibition. Phil Brandon, distiller and founder of Rock Town, has a key role in the day-to-day working of the distillery, making sure that every grain of corn, barley, wheat, and rye used to create any of the spirits is grown in Arkansas and sourced from within 125 miles of the distillery. This dedication to using locally sourced ingredients simply isn't possible for the large distillers and is one of the many unique selling points, not just for Rock Town, but for craft whiskey and spirits in general.

The flagship whiskeys from Rock Town consist of the Young Bourbon, Hickory Smoked Whiskey, and the Arkansas Rye. The bourbon has done extremely well since its launch, winning double gold medals in 2013 at the San Francisco World Spirits Competition, for Small Batch Bourbon in the ten years and younger category, as well as a gold medal in the same year at the World Whiskies Awards in London.

The Hickory Smoked Wheat Whiskey is particularly unusual; not only is it the only 100 percent wheat whiskey on the market, but the grain has been smoked in hickory smokers, lending a sweet, smoky flavor to the spirit. This experimental kind of whiskey is something you will rarely ever see from a large, well-established distillery, adding yet another string to the bow of craft distilling. The Arkansas Rye Whiskey is the latest addition to the collection, launched in fall 2013. Alongside their three whiskeys, a collection of fruit-infused liqueurs can be found, as well as a vodka and a gin.

WHAT THEY SAY ...

"Yes, honey ... just squeeze your rage up into a bitter little ball and release it at an appropriate time, like that day I hit the referee with the whiskey bottle."

—Homer Simpson

Arkansas Rye Whiskey

A bold spicy whiskey with intense oak spice and notes of mint chocolate chip ice cream.

★ ABV: 46% ★ Type: Rye
★ Region: New York

Arkansas Hickory Smoked Whiskey

Light and sweet, with a creamy mouthfeel and notes of vanilla, soft smoke, and biscuit.

★ ABV: 46% ★ Type: Corn
★ Region: New York

Al Capone's whiskey

Despite the ban on alcohol during Prohibition from 1920 to 1933, the era was a boom time for many. Scottish whisky producers gained a foothold in the United States market, and bootleggers such as Al Capone made fortunes.

As well as importing illicit alcohol, Capone also sourced illegally produced whiskey from the United States. One favored supplier was the small town of Templeton in Iowa, where local farmers produced a quality rye whiskey that was christened "the Good Stuff."

Capone shipped barrels of it all over the United States, and legend has it that bottles were even smuggled into the cell of prisoner AZ-85 in Alcatraz.

When Prohibition ended, the farmers went back to producing the odd batch for themselves and loyal customers—still on an illegal basis. However, in 2001 the recipe was revived by Scott Bush and Meryl Kerkhoff, descendants of the original makers, and 68 legitimate barrels were produced. After aging, the first bottles were available in 2006.

Based on the original Prohibition-era recipe and aged in charred new oak barrels, Templeton Rye has a dry, grassy,

Christmas-spice aroma, with hints of caramel, butterscotch, and allspice, and a smooth finish.

The small-batch production process has led to a lauded whiskey, which picked up the 2008 Los Angeles International Wine & Spirit Competition gold medal in the American Straight Rye category. In December 2013 the distillery sold its millionth bottle.

Smooth Ambler

Smooth Ambler distillery was built in 2009 in Maxwelton, West Virginia. The project was spearheaded by distillery founders, Tinsley Azariah "Tag" Galyean and John Little, who, after the economic downturn in 2008, had decided to start a craft distillery. Like other grain-to-glass craft distillers, the Smooth Ambler team have made the distillery pay by producing gin and vodka, but they also sought out a number of casks in order to blend a series of small-batch bourbons and ryes, which they sell under the name Old Scout. There are currently four whiskeys available under the Old Scout name; these include a 7-year-old rye whiskey and three bourbons, a 7-year-old, 10-year-old, and a limited release called Yearling.

Old Scout, 7-Year-Old Bourbon

A big, spicy bourbon with a high rye content of 36 percent and bags of character. Baked apples dusted with cinnamon, with toasted almonds and a fresh, minty feel.

✹ ABV: 49.5% ✹ TYPE: Bourbon ✹ REGION: West Virginia

Stranahan's

The Stranahan's distillery was founded in 2003 by whiskey enthusiasts Jess Graber and George Stranahan, and upon its completion became the first legal whiskey distillery to be built in Colorado. Since its inception the distillery has gone from strength to strength and in 2010 caught the eye of New York spirits company, Proximo Spirits. Since coming under the wing of Proximo the distillery has undergone a significant expansion, and in the coming years should have enough mature stock to sustain a significant distribution network around the globe. Stranahan's is unusual among United States distillers in that it focuses entirely on making malt whiskey. Each release is made in small batches of 5,000 bottles, from casks between two and five years old. The distillery has just the one core bottling, but a single-barrel release called Snowflake is released once a year.

Colorado

Big, spicy, and takes no prisoners. Caramel, vanilla, green fruit, nutmeg, woody spice, and subtle citrus.

✲ ABV: 47% ✲ TYPE: Single Malt ✲ REGION: Colorado

Copper Fox

The Copper Fox distillery is located at the foot of the Blue Ridge Mountains in Sperryville, Virginia. The company was founded in 2000 by Rick Wasmund. Rick had spent the previous years honing his skills and ideas while visiting a huge number of distilleries around the United States and Scotland, including six weeks working at the famous Bowmore distillery on Islay. This time studying whiskey production and the various methods used in both countries would prove to be invaluable to Rick in making a good-quality spirit from the very start of his project.

The distillery in Sperryville was built in 2005, with the first spirit running from its stills in 2006, although previous releases of Wasmund's whiskey had been produced at another facility. Unlike most U.S. distillers, Wasmund's puts a lot of focus on making single malt whiskey and is one of only a handful of distilleries in the world that malt their own barley. The first stages of the malting are undertaken in a traditional fashion, but in the final stage of drying—rather than use peat, warm air, or a smokeless fuel—they use fruitwood chips, such as apple or cherry, to imbue the grain with a unique smokiness. Unusual smoking techniques are becoming more commonplace among America's craft distillers, whereas in Scotland these techniques cannot be employed by law. Maturation at Copper Fox takes place in charred oak casks, and the process is supplemented by the addition of fruitwood chips to add more distinctive and unusual flavors to the spirit. The use of chipping in maturation has certainly raised a few eyebrows, as it is not common practice in whiskey maturation.

Wasmund's Single Malt— Aged for 42 months

Plenty going on for a relatively young malt whiskey. Sweet, fruity, and spicy, with a hint of pepper, orange zest, and woody spice.

★ ABV: 48% ★ Type: Single Malt ★ Region: Virginia

Copper Fox Rye— Aged for 12 months

Made with two thirds rye and one third malted barley and aged in second-fill bourbon casks. Toasted rye bread, vanilla ice cream, honey, figs, and roasted hazelnuts abound.

★ ABV: 45% ★ Type: Rye ★ Region: Virginia

CANADA

Settlers in what was then known as New France started distilling their own spirits as early as 1668, under colonial administrator Jean Talon. The first Canadian distillery was opened in Quebec City in 1769, and by the 1840s there were more than 200 in operation.

Canadian whisky is generally a multigrain blended style of whisky that is smoother, sweeter, and lighter than other styles. To qualify as Canadian whisky it must be produced and aged in Canada for at least three years in wooden barrels, and be at least 40 percent ABV.

The whisky is colloquially known as rye; however,

it is seldom made from 100 percent rye. The early settlers grew rye grain because it thrived in poor soil, so they used it to make whisky. They shifted to distilling with wheat when it became the principal grain of the prairies, although they retained some rye as a flavoring agent. This practice persisted when distillers switched to corn as their main grain.

Canadian whisky saw strong growth in the nineteenth century, with entrepreneurs such as Hiram Walker, founder of Canadian Club, and Gooderham and Worts producing whisky on an industrial scale. Their products found a ready market in the United States, where Canadian whisky had such a high

Canadian whisky saw strong growth in the nineteenth century.

reputation that some local producers tried to pass their whiskey off as Canadian.

Some hold that Canadian distillers benefited from Prohibition in the United States, but Canada also had a brief period of prohibition, although it did not overlap with that of the United States. Ironically today smuggling from the United States into Canada is a problem due to the disparity on alcohol duties.

Although Canadian whisky's flavor profile makes it ideal for mixing, its reputation has suffered in recent years as some have labeled it as lacking in taste. However, the industry is fighting back with new straight rye, spiced, and small-batch whiskies. Connoisseur blends such as Lot 40, Forty Creek, and Century Reserve are helping Canadian whisky regain some of its reputation.

Alberta Premium

The Alberta distillery in Calgary has been making huge volumes of rye whisky for nearly 70 years, and unlike other distilleries in Canada and the United States it uses 100 percent rye. Although rye whisky is considered to be the "house style" whisky of Canada, in truth most Canadian whisky contains very little rye in the mash. Unlike the United States, where there must be a minimum percentage of 51 percent for whiskey to be called a rye whiskey, Canada has no such legal requirement, so many rye whiskies are in fact more corn-based than rye. Making rye whisky is notoriously difficult for distillers, with the sticky consistency of the mash often creating problems with equipment. However, with Alberta this is certainly not the case—the Alberta team are rye distilling experts, and aside from their own whiskies service the rye requirements of many other producers.

Made with 100 percent rye and aged for five years, this whisky has a very full flavor. Rye spice, honey, citrus zest, and vanilla toffee.

★ ABV: 40%

Canadian Club Classic

Without doubt this is one of the most iconic Canadian whiskies and also one of the most accessible in terms of price and availability. Canadian Club was first made available in 1858 and was one of few whiskies of that time that had matured over two years in oak. This made it significantly softer and easier to drink than many of its rivals, helping propel the whisky to success. The brand continued to grow even throughout Prohibition and is said to have been one of the main whiskies smuggled by infamous gangster Al Capone, who (if legend is to be believed) managed to buy a bottle of Canadian Club in Ontario for $7.75 and sell it in the United States for $75. Having been established for so many decades Canadian Club has enjoyed a rich and colorful history.

Spiced sweet fruit, buttery pastry, and caramel on the nose, with chocolate orange and toffee on the palate and finish.

★ ABV: 40%

Caribou Crossing

Caribou Crossing was the first release of a single-barrel Canadian whisky and is produced by the enormous Sazerac Company (owner of Buffalo Trace distillery). As well as producing a great many American whiskeys the company also produces no fewer than 24 Canadian brands. In order to create all these different Canadian whiskies, Sazerac has large stocks of Canadian whisky, said to be in the region of around 200,000 barrels. Therefore, when it comes to narrowing down a few casks for Caribou Crossing there are plenty to choose from, ensuring a quality whisky. Barrel selection is undertaken by Sazerac's master blender, Drew Mayville, and Caribou Crossing is likely to be followed by other, more premium releases. Since the first release of Caribou Crossing the whisky has received high praise from many critics.

Being single barrel, bottlings will vary from batch to batch. Soft and smooth, with crème brûlée, vanilla, tangerine, and a ryelike spiciness.

✴ ABV: 40%

Crown Royal Reserve

Crown Royal is undoubtedly one of the most iconic Canadian whiskies, and was once the jewel in the crown for the Seagram distillery. The whisky was first made in 1939 to mark the first royal tour of Canada by reigning British monarchs King George VI and Queen Elizabeth. Samuel Bronfman, the president of Seagram, decided to create a quality whisky to be packaged in a crown-shaped bottle and dressed in a royal purple bag. The brand's standout design soon caught the eye of the consumer and embedded itself as a premium product, which over the decades grew to become one of the best-known Canadian whiskies. In addition to the Reserve, whiskies from the Crown Royal range include the Deluxe, Black, Maple, XO, and Extra Rare.

This more recent release won a gold medal at the Canadian Whisky Awards in 2012. Soft and smooth, with notes of cinnamon, toffee, and caramel.

✴ ABV: 40%

Forty Creek Barrel Select

The Forty Creek distillery was founded in 1992 in Grimsby, Ontario, by a winemaker called John Hall. John was in the wine trade for 20 years before starting the Forty Creek distillery and has established his whisky as one of the rising stars of the Canadian whisky scene. Production at Forty Creek sets out to mirror a more traditional style of whisky making and uses two copper pot stills to create its spirit. Unlike many distilleries in the United States and Canada, Forty Creek believes that each grain type should be mashed and distilled separately rather than using a mash bill. The single-grain spirits are filled into a variety of different oak casks with varying origins and degrees of charring. The Forty Creek range is extensive and contains no fewer than nine expressions.

Aged between six and ten years in American white oak, then finished for six months in sherry casks. Rich, nutty, sweet, and spicy.

★ ABV: 40%

Gibson's 12-Year-Old

The Gibson's brand can trace its roots back to the mid-1800s, when John Gibson traveled from his Scottish homeland to Pennsylvania. Here John set up a distillery, and by the early 1900s had established one of the largest whiskey producing companies in the United States. However, the good times were not to last for the brand, and as Prohibition hit in the 1920s all maturing stock and distillery equipment were auctioned off and the distillery closed, never to reopen. That was until the 1970s, when the brand was revived by Schenley Distillers, which began making Gibson's whiskey at their distillery in Quebec. Over the last few decades the brand has reestablished itself and has become a huge hit in the domestic market. The range also includes Sterling, Grey Cup, and Rare releases.

Sadly, this release seems to be available only in Canada. A soft whisky with notes of vanilla, cloves, candy-coated almonds, and oaky spice.

★ ABV: 40%

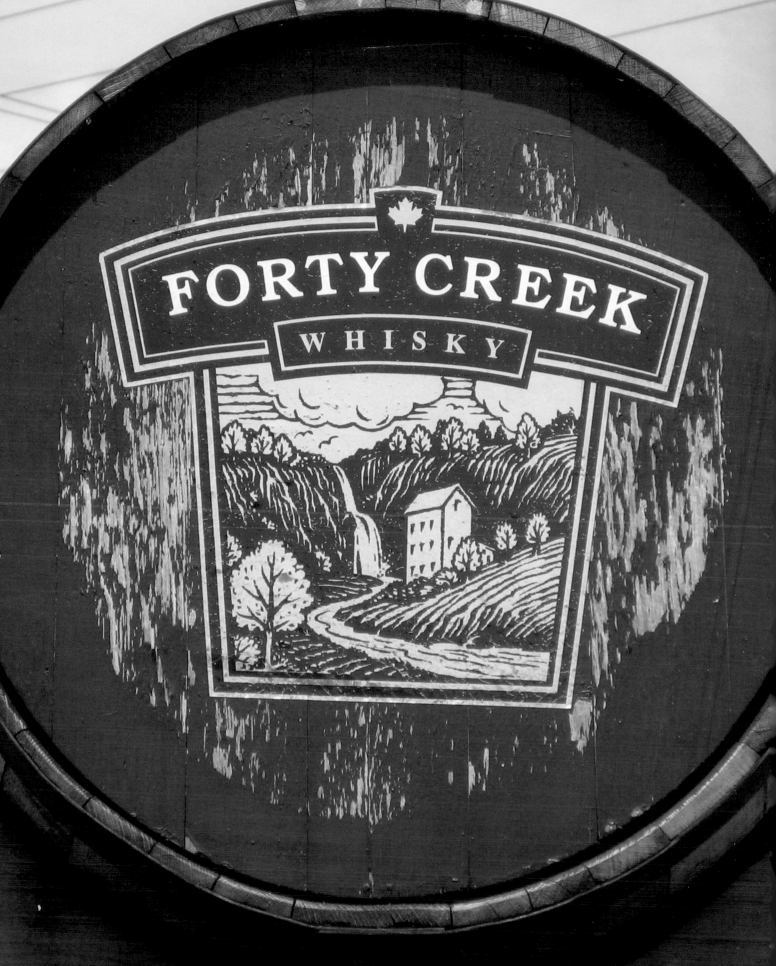

Seagram's VO

Seagram's VO was once one of the best-selling whiskies in the world and to this day is one of the oldest brands of Canadian whisky available. The Seagrams were a very influential distilling family and played a significant role in the history of Canadian whisky and a number of other distilleries around the world. This VO release was originally made by Joseph Seagram, who (if legend is to be believed) crafted the whisky from some of his finest stocks on the occasion of his son's wedding in 1913. This whisky was originally made at Seagram's Waterloo distillery, but since its closure in 1992 the brand has been made by Diageo at its distillery in Valleyfield, Quebec. The "VO" on the label simply stands for "Very Own." A handful of other Seagram's whiskies are available, including Seven Crown and Five Star Rye.

Used by most as a mixing whisky. Fruity, corny, plenty of spicy cinnamon, and a slight bitterness.

★ ABV: 40%

Stalk and Barrel Single Malt Cask Two

The Still Waters Distillery was set up in 2009 by Barry Bernstein and Barry Stein on the outskirts of Toronto, and was the first artisan or craft distiller to operate in Ontario. Compared to other Canadian distilleries Still Water is tiny and produces only two barrels of whisky a week. As a result, the distillery can be run almost completely as a two-man operation. Bernstein and Stein have a very hands-on approach and take care of nearly all the production, overseeing every stage from milling the grain through to hand-labeling the bottles. Four types of whisky are made at Still Waters: namely single malt, rye, corn, and blended. Each single-malt release is bottled from one single cask, with most bottled at cask strength. Stalk and Barrel Single Malt is made from 100 percent Canadian two-row malted barley, and as with all Still Water's whiskies has no added coloring and is not chill-filtered.

Seeing Canadian whisky at this strength is a rarity. Floral and sweet, with candied fruit, marzipan, and a biscuit taste.

★ ABV: 61.3%

WhistlePig Straight Rye

The WhistlePig brand is a more unusual Canadian whisky sourced by David Pickerell, who was previously the master distiller at Maker's Mark. David set out with a mission to find the best rye whisky available, and after 14 years his quest finally came to an end. The whisky David found is shrouded in mystery, and the distillery of origin remains undisclosed, but what is certain is that the whisky is made with 100 percent rye. This is particularly unusual as most high-percentage rye whiskies available are only 60–65 percent rye, with the other 35–40 percent being made up from corn or malted barley. This total absence of other grains in the mash makes for a unique offering. Another unusual point is that the whisky is not bottled at source but at the WhistlePig farm in Vermont.

Definitely not for the fainthearted, the gloves are off with this one. Licorice, oak, menthol, and intense spice are dominant.

★ ABV: 50%

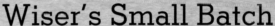

Wiser's Small Batch

The original Wiser's distillery operated in Prescott, where the reputation of this whisky was forged by the owner, John Phillip Wiser. John is regarded by many as one of the pioneers of Canadian whisky and helped shape and define the Canadian whisky category. Sadly only six years after his death in 1911 the company was sold to Corby's Distilleries Ltd., which soon moved the brand to its company in Corbyville, Ontario. Eventually this distillery also faced closure and the whisky moved again to its current home in Walkerville at the Hiram Walker Distillery. Here the whisky is made to the exact same recipe and specifications mapped out by John Wiser all those years ago. The current Wiser's range also includes Special Blend, Deluxe, Spiced, Legacy, and an 18-year-old.

Small Batch

A more premium release of Wiser's, with notes of dark fruit, pepper, apricot, vanilla, and oaky spice.

★ ABV: 43.4%

JAPAN

Despite being a relative newcomer to whiskey making, Japan is now the second-biggest producer of single malt whiskey in the world.

Japan's ranking among whiskey nations recently rose when Suntory bought Jim Beam for $16 billion. The deal makes Suntory the third largest spirits company in the world. As well as acquiring the world's biggest-selling bourbon, it also now owns Teacher's, Laphroaig, and Canadian Club.

It's the latest chapter in the story of a long love affair with whiskey. It started in 1854, when Commodore Matthew Perry, the American commander who negotiated the treaty to open up Japanese trade to the West, brought 110 gallons of whiskey as a gift for the emperor. Inventive Japanese drinks makers tried to replicate the taste of foreign liquor, initially without great success. Spirit known as *yoshu* was distilled as early as 1870, but commercial production of Japanese whisky did not commence until 1924. This was when Shinjiro Torii established Kotobukiya Limited—later renamed Suntory—the first distillery in Japan, located in the Vale of Yamazaki.

Torii hired another Japanese whisky pioneer, Masataka Taketsuru, to help him. Taketsuru had traveled to Scotland in 1918 to study the secrets of making whisky, and would eventually strike out on his own in 1934, when he founded Dai Nippon Kaju, literally "The Great Japan Juice Company," with a distillery at Yoichi on Hokkaido. This would later become Nikka, which produces brands such as Black Nikka, Nikka Single Cask, and Yoichi 20-year-old, which was voted World's Best Single Malt at the World Whiskies Awards in 2008.

The Scottish influence on Japanese whisky making, which began with the dedicated studies of Masataka Taketsuru, continues to this day, and the Japanese spell "whisky" the Scottish way. Distilleries use malted barley rather than corn or rye, and whiskies are crafted in a Scottish style that echoes Lowland and Speyside varieties. They generally avoid the heavy smoke, peat, and saline flavors of Islay and Campbeltown. Japanese oak, also known as Mizunara oak, is unique to Japanese whisky production and is used in a handful of whiskies to create rich fruit flavors, not dissimilar to those of European oak.

SUNTORY YAMAZAKI DISTILLERY

THE YAMAZAKI SINGLE MALT WHISKY 山崎

Although initially Japanese whisky was produced for the home market, in recent years it has been increasingly lauded as world class. Today, Japanese whiskies are popular as a style of their own and exports have increased.

Japan's distilleries' attention to detail has helped them win a barrelful of top international awards. Suntory's top-of-the-line Yamazaki 25-Year-Old—which, if you can find it, costs upward of $1,350 a bottle—was named World's Best Single Malt at *Whisky Magazine*'s 2012 World Whiskies Awards in London. Nikka's Yoichi single malt has also won prestigious

awards, and Suntory's Hibiki 30-Year-Old was named World's Best Blended Whisky at the World Whiskies Awards in 2008. Suntory's Hibiki 21-Year-Old took the blended category trophy at the U.K.'s 2013 International Spirits Challenge, where Suntory was named Distiller of the Year for the third time. Japanese single malts have even outperformed their Scottish counterparts in blind tastings in the recent past.

Part of the reason may be that Japanese distillers have had to be more experimental in order to produce better blended whisky. In Scotland, blends are created by bringing together different malts from

Japan's distilleries' attention to detail has helped them win a barrelful of top international awards.

an array of distilleries to produce the perfect whisky. In Japan, companies are reluctant to trade with their competitors, so a blended whisky will generally only contain malt whisky from their own distilleries, sometimes supplemented with imported Scottish malts. As a reaction to this, individual distilleries in Japan are adept at producing a more diverse range of whiskies.

When it comes to drinking whisky, the Japanese are keen on pairing it with food. Usually this is done in the form of a watered whisky or a highball, an easy-to-drink concoction of one part whisky and two to three parts soda water. It has become so commonplace that it is sold in cans in convenience stores and on draft in bars as an alternative to beer. Different whiskies can be matched with different courses, including sushi, sashimi, tempura, and even sweet courses.

Single malt is typically served on ice, but not just any ice. Connoisseurs will seek out a bar where the bartender is adept at serving whisky with an ice ball. This is a large ball of ice that chills the whisky without overdiluting it. The bartender carves the ice ball, and puts it into a glass of water to cool the glass. The water is then discarded and the bartender pours whisky on top of the ball and rolls it to homogenize the temperature. The Japanese are nothing if not obsessive about detail.

Chichibu

Chichibu was the first distillery to be built in Japan since the 1970s. It was founded in 2008, making it Japan's youngest distillery. The distillery resides in the town of Chichibu, close to the city of Satima, northwest of Tokyo. The distillery was set up by Ichiro Akuto, grandson of the owner of Hanyu distillery, which was dismantled in 2004. Ichiro acquired the remaining casks and released a celebrated range of whiskies under the name Ichiro's Malt, making a name for himself among Japanese whisky fans of the world. The Chichibu distillery is a small operation and will eventually be capable of taking every stage of production in-house, with plans under way to do its own malting, peating, coopering, and bottling on site. Around ten percent of the barley used is grown locally, and maturation takes place in many cask types, including Mizunara (Japanese oak) casks. The distillery makes both peated and unpeated spirit and has released a handful of limited expressions.

2009 The Floor Malted

A lively young whisky showing plenty of promise. Notes of vanilla ice cream, oaky spice, and a buttery sweetness.

✶ ABV: 50.5% ✶ TYPE: Single Malt

Lost in Translation

For those in search of the perfect setting to sample a Japanese whisky, there can be only one venue: the New York Bar in the Park Hyatt Tokyo hotel. It was here that many of the scenes of the Oscar-nominated movie *Lost in Translation* were shot.

Located on the 52nd floor of the hotel, the bar offers breathtaking views of the city, especially if you can grab one of the high stools situated at the bar. However it is unlikely that you will experience the sort of moody solitude that Bill Murray's character enjoys in the Sofia Coppola movie, as it is now an established stop on the tourist trail.

Bar staff will helpfully point out that in the movie, Murray's character drinks Suntory Hibiki Whisky, but the drinks menu has many other brands. The Hibiki 17-year-old picked up the World Whiskies Award for Best Japanese Blended Whisky in 2012.

For drinkers more in search of a dram than cinematic ambience, Tokyo has many specialist whisky bars, often with hundreds of different brands on offer. Recommendations include the Shot Bar Zoetrope, which mixes an enviable selection of whiskies with black-and-white classic movies; the homage to Caledonia vibe of The Helmsdale, and Campbeltown Loch, which boasts a rotating selection of around 250 whiskies, including many rare gems from the 1970s and 1980s.

Hakushu

The Hakushu distillery was founded in 1973 by Suntory, and was built to cater for a whisky boom that followed World War II and to take pressure off the aging Yamazaki distillery. Standing at 2,300 feet (700 meters) above sea level and nestled in deep, dense forest in the foothills of Mount Kai-Komagatake, the distillery is the most remote in Japan. When first built, Hakushu was the largest distillery in the world, operating a total of 36 stills and with a production capacity exceeding any distillery in Scotland, Canada, or the United States.

During the 1980s, Japan, like Scotland, saw a whisky recession that led to the closure of half the Hakushu distillery and a reduction in size to 12 stills. Currently the world is seeing another boom period for whisky, and once again Hakushu is expanding. Four new washbacks were installed in 2012, and more recently the distillery has been fitted with the equipment necessary to make grain whisky. Hakushu's main purpose is to make peated malt whisky for use in Suntory's blending programs, and like Yamazaki it is capable of making various styles of malt by utilizing a variety of pot stills. This ability to make different styles of spirit is essential, as trading between rival distilleries in Japan is nonexistent. Maturation at Hakushu takes place mainly in ex-bourbon casks, but sherry casks are also filled. Over the years the Hakushu range has seen a plethora of awards and is widely available. The core range from Hakushu includes 12-, 18-, and 25-year-olds, but like Yamazaki, limited releases are numerous and appear regularly.

12-Year-Old

Light and fresh with a stone, mineral quality. Notes of diced apple and pear, with custard creams and subtle smoke.

✳ ABV: 43% ✳ Type: Single Malt

Bourbon Barrel

Matured in first-fill bourbon casks and with a higher ABV, this expression has more clout than the 12-year-old. Bursting with vanilla and fruit with a creamy sweetness and traces of peat.

✳ ABV: 48.2% ✳ Type: Single Malt

Hibiki 12

Incredibly soft and easy-drinking and said to contain whiskies up to 30 years old. Notes of honey, plum jelly, subtle vanilla, and caramel.

✶ ABV: 43% ✶ TYPE: Blended

Hibiki 17

Mellow, soft, and silky, with notes of lemon and lime candies, cinnamon, hints of cocoa, and traces of spicy fruit and smoke on the finish.

✶ ABV: 43% ✶ TYPE: Blended

Hibiki

Hibiki is the flagship brand of the Suntory company and was launched in 1989 to commemorate the 90th anniversary of the company. The brand was relatively unknown outside Japan, but in the 2000s this was set to change. In 2003 the whisky featured heavily in the movie *Lost in Translation*, which starred Bill Murray and Scarlet Johansson. This exposure did the brand no harm and certainly raised its profile; however, it was in 2008 that the brand really took off, when a 30-year-old Hibiki won the "World's Best Blended Whisky" category at the World Whiskies Awards in London. This was the first time a Japanese whisky had won a prize of this magnitude, and as a result the blend caught the attention of many aficionados around the globe.

Since then, the brand has grown and boasts an impressive trophy cabinet, with many awards from various spirit competitions. The blend is made using whisky from Suntory's distilleries, with the malt whisky coming from the Yamazaki and Hakushu distilleries and grain whisky coming from Chita distillery. Maturation takes place in a variety of cask types, including casks that previously held a Japanese plum liqueur known as Umeshu. The Hibiki blends are a far cry from typical blended whisky and offer a stunning range of flavors, being exceptionally well constructed by Suntory's master blenders. Hibiki is bottled in a distinctive decanter-style bottle that has 24 facets representing the 24 seasons in the old Japanese lunar calendar. The Japanese word *hibiki* translates as "harmony." The current Hibiki range consists of 12-, 17-, 21-, and 30-year-olds.

Nikka

The Nikka whisky company was founded in 1934 by Masataka Taketsuru, who is widely accepted as the father of Japanese whisky. Masataka was born in Takehara, a coastal town located around 40 miles (65 km) from Hiroshima City. The Taketsuru family had been making sake at their brewery since 1733, and Masataka was set to take over the reins, but first he had to learn the art of brewing and no small amount of chemistry. In 1918 he set off for Scotland, where he studied chemistry at the University of Glasgow, furthering the knowledge and understanding of brewing that he had learned back home. It was here that whisky captured his heart and mind, and he set about learning the art of whisky making.

This was by no means an easy task, as many distilleries refused to offer him an apprenticeship, but eventually he was taken in by a handful of distilleries, including Calder and the now closed Hazelburn distillery in Campbeltown. These distilleries welcomed the young chemist with open arms, and by 1920 Masataka had learned the skills needed to make both malt and grain whisky.

But the knowledge of whisky making was not all he acquired in Scotland, as it was during this time that he met his wife, Jessie Roberta Cowan, known as Rita, and after living together in Campbeltown the pair journeyed back to Japan. On his return Masataka teamed up with Shinjiro Torii (founder of Suntory), and in 1923 they set about the creation of Japan's first malt whisky at the Yamazaki distillery.

After a number of years with the young Suntory company, Masataka took the decision to set up independently, and in 1934 he founded the Yoichi distillery in the north of Japan, releasing the first Nikka whisky in 1940. The distillery was built in a remote location, which was impractical from a logistical standpoint. But Masataka was a devout believer that the environment in which a whisky was made and matured was a key factor in its quality, and although impractical the climate was much the same as the areas in Scotland where he had served his apprenticeships.

In 1969 Nikka's second distillery, Miyagikyo, was built near the city of Sendai to help deal with the increasing demand. In August 1979 Masataka died and was buried next to his wife in Yoichi. Today the company is the second-largest drinks company in Japan and owns the Ben Nevis distillery in Scotland, near where Masataka studied all those years ago. The Nikka range of whiskies is extensive and includes a range of single malts from both distilleries, as well as a range of blended malts.

Taketsuru 17-Year-Old

Dried stone fruit and pipe tobacco on the nose, with baked apples and cinnamon and mocha on the palate and finish.

★ ABV: 43% ★ TYPE: Blended Malt

Nikka Coffey Grain

Soft cocoa and caramel on the nose, with vanilla custard and wafer on the palate, leading to sweet vanilla and cherry and almond tart finish.

★ ABV: 45% ★ TYPE: Grain

Nikka from the Barrel

Bold and spicy, with notes of cocoa, fresh orchard fruit, hard candies, and a trace of smoke.

★ ABV: 51.4% ★ TYPE: Blended

Yamazaki

The whisky from the Yamazaki distillery is probably the best known of the Japanese whiskies and is available all around the world. The distillery is owned by the giant drinks company Suntory, which as of early 2014 became the third-largest drinks company in the world, owning distilleries in many whisky-producing countries. Yamazaki is Japan's oldest purpose-built whisky distillery and was established in 1923 by the founder of Suntory, Shinjiro Torii. The distillery is located in the Vale of Yamazaki on the outskirts of Kyoto in the heart of Japan.

As well as being the oldest whisky distillery in Japan, Yamazaki is one of the largest, producing an estimated 1.5–2 million gallons (6–7 million liters) of spirit each year. The distillery has a total of 12 stills of varying shapes and sizes, which allows it to make the many different spirit styles needed to construct the blends within the Suntory portfolio. Most malt needed for production is imported from a variety of sources, including Europe and the United States, although some is sourced locally. Casks for maturation are also imported, with ex-bourbon casks coming from the United States and ex-sherry casks coming from Spain. Around the time of World War II, a shortage of sherry casks resulted in the distillery sourcing casks made from Japan's native oak, called Mizunara. These native casks are still filled today and lend similar flavors to those of European oak. The core malt whiskies from Yamazaki include 12-, 15-, 25-, 35-, and 50-year-olds. Limited releases are numerous and are released regularly.

12-Year-Old

A full-bodied, rich fruity whisky with notes of orange marmalade, custard cream cookies, vanilla, and soft, oaky spice.

★ ABV: 43% ★ TYPE: Single Malt

18-Year-Old

Rich and complex with a soft mouthfeel and a multitude of dark fruit flavors balanced with traces of dark chocolate and maraschino cherries.

★ ABV: 43% ★ TYPE: Single Malt

Yoichi

Yoichi is the most northerly distillery in Japan and the only distillery on the island of Hokkaido. The distillery was founded in 1934 by Masataka Taketsuru after he left the Yamazaki distillery and Suntory. The distillery is the realization of Masataka's ideals of whisky making and mirrors beautifully the methods he observed while learning his art in Scotland. The distillery operates three pairs of stills, all of which are direct-fired, meaning they are heated with coal, as opposed to indirect-fired stills, which are heated by steam coils. This method of firing was once commonplace in Scotland, but over the years direct-fired stills have become extinct, with the last being removed from Glendronach in 2005. Yoichi also produces whiskies with various levels of peat, from totally unpeated to heavily peated. As well as using these traditional methods the distillery has on-site coopers making

casks. All these factors combine to make Yoichi the most traditional distillery in Japan—in many ways more traditional than most in Scotland.

The first single malt from Yoichi was released in 1984 as a 12-year-old and was sold under the name Hokkaido, which was once the name of the distillery. In 2008 Yoichi made headlines around the world when a 20-year-old expression won "World's Best Single Malt Whisky" at the World Whiskies Awards in London. This created a huge buzz around Japanese whisky and had enthusiasts the world over trying to seek out the winning whisky.

Maturation at Yoichi takes place in a number of cask types, including virgin oak casks made by the distillery's coopers. The core range consists of NAS and 10-, 12-, 15-, and 20-year-olds, and a number of single-cask releases can also be found.

15-Year-Old

A deep complex whisky with notes of ripe berries, gingerbread, cocoa, Fig Newtons, subtle smoke, and traces of peat.

★ ABV: 45% ★ TYPE: Single Malt

10-Year-Old

Light and fresh, with subtle peat on the nose and notes of honey, vanilla, oak, and fruit on the palate and finish.

★ ABV: 45% ★ TYPE: Single Malt

REST OF THE WORLD

For many years whiskey has been enjoyed around the world, but only produced in Scotland, Ireland, America, and Canada, with Japan a recent plus-one.

In recent years that picture has started to change dramatically, as countries that have always enjoyed a dram have started to produce their own. Some are British expat hotspots such as India, South Africa, and Australia, where it is understandable that a historical connection is being pursued. But many of the new whiskey producers have no such history.

From France and Finland to Taiwan and Tasmania, whiskey distilleries are cropping up around the world in places that you might not expect. In some ways the profusion is perhaps not that surprising. After all, whiskey has long been the world's favorite dark spirit, with a tumbler of Scotch, rye, or bourbon being enjoyed from Carnoustie to Cape Town. The Scotch Whisky Association places the value of its exports at £4.23 billion ($7 billion), while world retail sales of whiskey are valued at $41.7 billion.

Just as the craft beer movement has spread around the world, whiskey making is now being attempted by global whiskey aficionados. The results are fascinating, because although the basic process of distilling is the same the world over, new producers are doing things their own way, and in the process are coming up with new tastes and expressions.

In the not-too-distant past, a list of the top 100 whiskeys would have been dominated by Scotch whisky, with a few other names from the major whiskey producers. Although Scotch still sets a benchmark, the rest of the world is catching up quickly, and new whiskeys are increasingly hailed as the equal of, if not superior to, Old World whiskey.

All of this is good news for a drink that is perennially in danger of becoming associated with an aging consumer base if it does not move with the times.

New whiskeys have used innovative packaging and processes to come up with imaginative new spirits.

Budding whiskey manufacturers have realized that there is no point trying to produce a facsimile of Scotch single malt, as this would doom them to failure. Instead, companies like Mackmyra have purposely tried to do something that is quite different—for example using juniper branches and peat to malt barley, aping the use of juniper in Swedish cuisine. They have also experimented with the use of fresh Swedish oak barrels.

Welsh whiskey producer Penderyn uses a single-still system designed by David Faraday, a descendant of

the Victorian scientist Michael Faraday. While most Scottish and Irish distilleries use a conventional two- or three-pot still system, the technology developed at Penderyn allows an extremely clean, flavorful spirit to be produced from a single still. The barley wash is supplied by Welsh brewer Brains, and the spirit is aged in Buffalo Trace bourbon casks before finishing in Madeira, sherry, port, or old Islay whisky barrels.

Different climates are also helping new whiskey producers to come up with different flavors.

Making whiskey is not for those with a short-term mentality. Some of the best whiskeys in the world were laid down 40 or 50 years ago.

The high temperatures in India and Australia help whiskey mature at a much faster rate. As well as leading to interesting new flavor profiles, this holds out the prospect of whiskey producers in these countries being able to get their product to market more quickly. Whiskey is a long-term investment, and the earlier producers can start to make a return on their money, the more likely they are to remain competitive.

Financial constraints haven't stopped new enthusiasts coming on board. One of the latest is Puni distillery in the north of Italy. The family-owned company started making spirits in 2012 and expects to have its first whiskey bottled by 2015. In true Italian fashion, the distillery is something of a design statement, housed in a 43-foot (13-meter) tall redbrick

cube designed by architect Werner Tscholl. Puni is using three cereals: barley, rye, and wheat, for its whiskey, which is matured in bourbon, Marsala, and wine casks inside an old World War II bunker.

Other projects have been spotted in Argentina, where two microdistilleries are envisaged in Patagonia. The first, La Alazana, started in 2011, and hopes to have whiskey ready by late 2014. Another, La Patagonia, is still in the pipeline. Israel's Milk and Honey distillery has raised more than $1 million to produce single malt whiskey by the Dead Sea.

Meanwhile New Zealand bottler Thomson Whisky is taking the step up to distilling its own spirit.

Making whiskey is not for those with a short-term mentality. Some of the best whiskeys in the world were laid down 40 or 50 years ago by people who may never have sampled them when they were bottled. New whiskey makers around the world are at the start of a long journey, during which they will make many discoveries and some mistakes. The more they learn about their craft, the better the results. With whiskey, time is a vital ingredient.

EUROPE

Europe has always been an important market for Scotch whisky, particularly in recent years as the drink is in long-term decline in its home market.

Now Europeans are starting to produce their own versions of one of their favorite drinks. New distillers are springing up all over Europe, from England and Wales through France and down to Spain. There is even a whiskey distillery in Switzerland.

Most are small and some have distilled previously or continue to distill other spirits. Others jumped in at the deep end with no previous experience. The whiskeys are generally produced for the local market, but some are expanding their ranges and looking to export.

Although most of the European players are fairly new, some have a longer history, such as Spain's Destilerias y Crianza del Whisky (DYC). It started producing whiskey in 1959 and is now the best-selling brand in its home market, with production of 610,000 gallons (2.3 million liters) a year. It also offers single malts.

Most European distilleries are not on the same scale, but their ambitions of producing a quality whiskey are equally serious. England's St. George's distillery opened in 2006, with its first release—or Chapter, as it calls them—in 2010. To date it has produced 13 small-batch chapters, picking up numerous awards along the way.

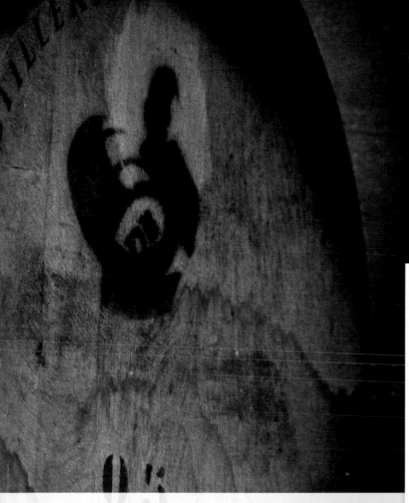

New distillers are springing up all over Europe, from England and Wales through France and down to Spain.

Sweden's Mackmyra is one of the best examples of European whiskey made good. It commenced production of malt whiskey in 1999 and now has several expressions available. In 2012 it was named European Spirits Producer in the International Wine and Spirit Competition in London. The company has floated on the Swedish stock exchange and moved to a new distillery with a capacity of 265,000 gallons (one million liters).

And new microdistilleries continue to pop up. In 2013, the first whiskey distillery in London for more than a century began production. Drinkers can expect to sample the first dram from the London Distillery Company, a fruity, light number with malt, chocolate, and caramel notes, by Christmas 2016.

St. George's

When St. George's distillery began to make its new-make spirit in 2006, it was the first whiskey distillery in England in over 100 years. The distillery was set up by father-and-son duo James and Andrew Nelstrop near the town of Thetford in Norfolk. It makes single malt whiskey of both a peated and unpeated variety, and ages mostly in ex-bourbon barrels from Buffalo Trace, although it does fill other types of casks on occasion, including wine, port, rum, and sherry.

The distillery takes care of every step of production, with milling, fermentation, distillation, maturation, bottling, and labeling all undertaken on site. The majority of bottlings from the distillery so far have been released in a series of Chapters, which have followed the spirit since its conception and showcase the evolution of the whiskey. Chapters 1–4 were bottled early on for those keen to try the peated and unpeated new-make spirit and the spirit after 18 months in cask. The first actual whiskey came along in 2009 as a limited release in Chapter 5, and was soon followed by the more widely available Chapter 6.

Over time other Chapters were released, some being heavily peated and others being matured in different types of cask. Of all the releases so far, Chapters 6, 9, and 11 have become the most widely available. Aside from the Chapters a number of limited expressions for various royal occasions have been released, and in 2013 the Black Range was introduced, with a view to establishing a more consistent product for wider release and for export. St. George's has firmly established itself as a respected whiskey producer and its whiskeys are sold by spirit specialists around the world.

Chapter 6

An unpeated expression bottled from ex-bourbon casks. Light and fresh, with green fruit, citrus, and subtle vanilla notes.

★ ABV: 46% ★ Type: Single Malt
★ Country: England

Chapter 11

A heavily peated expression bottled from ex-bourbon casks. Bonfire smoke and ash accompanied by ginger, pepper, and a trace of tropical fruit.

★ ABV: 46% ★ Type: Single Malt
★ Country: England

Adnams

The Adnams brewery was established in 1872 and has been making beer for nearly 150 years on the Suffolk coast at Southwold. In more recent years another string has been added to its bow: distillation and spirit production. The stillhouse at Adnams was built in 2010, and soon after its inauguration casks of whiskey were laid down to sleep, ready to be released in 2013 after their obligatory three years of maturation. Two inaugural whiskeys have been released, the first being a single malt made from East Anglian barley and aged in new French oak. The second is called Triple Grain and is a combination of malted barley, wheat, and oats aged in new American oak. Alongside whiskey the Adnams team make a variety of other spirits, including gin, vodka, and absinthe.

Single Malt Whisky No. 1

Young and feisty but a great start. Honey, stone fruit, vanilla, butterscotch, and a candied sweetness.

★ ABV: 43% ★ TYPE: Single Malt ★ COUNTRY: England

Penderyn

Penderyn is the only distillery in Wales, and can be found in the village of Penderyn, which lies in the southern reaches of the Brecon Beacons National Park. The distillery operates an unusual type of column still, which is not common practice in malt whiskey production and creates a far stronger new-make spirit than traditional pot stills.

The first single malt whiskey from Penderyn distillery was launched on St. David's Day, March 1, 2004, by H.R.H. Prince Charles, and was met with high praise from critics. Penderyn's standard release uses two types of casks. Primary maturation takes place in ex-bourbon barrels; this is followed by a period of extra maturation in Madeira casks. The Madeira adds an extra fruitiness to the spirit and helps soften it. The core releases consist of Madeira, Sherrywood, and a peated expression, all of which have won awards.

Madeira

A light and easygoing whiskey, with notes of vanilla, dried apricot, nectarine, raisins, and toffee.

★ ABV: 46% ★ TYPE: Single Malt ★ COUNTRY: Wales

The Belgian Owl

The Belgian Owl distillery was set up in 1997 by Etienne Bouillon and his two partners, and is located in the town of Grâce Hollogne, near the city of Liège. The first spirit from the distillery flowed in 2004, and in October 2007 Belgium had its very first malt whiskey. The first commercial release came in November 2008, followed by a 44-month-old limited release in 2009. A medley of cask-strength releases have appeared in the years since, with several new three- and four-year-old expressions appearing in 2013. The distillery operates on the outskirts of the town and uses locally grown barley in production. An unusual quirk of the distillery is that it is fitted with two secondhand pot stills that were acquired from the closed Speyside distillery, Caperdonich.

Belgian Owl Single Malt Whisky

Matured in American oak casks and bottled at three years, with notes of ripe apple and pear, ginger, vanilla, and hints of citrus.

✴ ABV: 46% ✴ TYPE: Single Malt ✴ COUNTRY: Belgium

Slyrs

The Slyrs distillery, as it is now known, was first built in 1928, and for many decades produced brandy under the name Lantenhammer in Schliersee, Bavaria. In 1999, the distillery changed direction and began to produce whiskey. By 2002 the whiskey had come of age and made its debut release, and in 2004 the distillery was rechristened with its current name, Slyrs. The malted barley used at the distillery is sourced locally, and rather unusually for whiskey, is smoked with beech wood. Another oddity at Slyrs is that maturation takes place in virgin 59-gallon (225-liter) casks made of American oak. Virgin oak casks are not commonplace in malt whiskey production and impart a lot of flavor to the spirit. Sherry and port casks are also used to create a diverse range, consisting of eight different whiskeys.

Slyrs

The starting point in the Slyrs range and bottled at three years old. Notes of vanilla, baked apples, cinnamon, citrus, and tree sap.

✴ ABV: 43% ✴ TYPE: Single Malt ✴ COUNTRY: Germany

Waldviertler Roggenhof

In 1995 Johann and Monika Haider began to make whiskey in the remote village of Roggenreith in Northern Austria, after founding the country's first whiskey distillery. The main type of whiskey made at Waldviertler is rye, which is sourced locally and has been grown in the area for so long that the village takes its name from the grain. As well as using locally sourced rye the distillery also uses locally sourced Austrian oak for its casks. The Waldviertler distillery is also home to a top-class visitor center called the Whisky World of Experience, which attracts around 75,000 visitors a year to the remote area. Peated and unpeated malt whiskeys are also made at the distillery as well as a large selection of rye styles, most of which are bottled as single cask.

Original Rye

Made with 60 percent rye and 40 percent malted barley, with notes of honey, vanilla, orange marmalade, and milk chocolate.

⁕ ABV: 41% ⁕ Type: Rye ⁕ Country: Austria

Zuidam

The Zuidam distillery resides in the small town of Baarle Nassau in the Netherlands. The company began in 1975 as a traditional family distillery, producing a range of spirits including vodka and genever. It wasn't until 2002 that the company decided to take the plunge into whiskey distilling, and in 2007 it released its first whiskey, a five-year-old single malt called Millstone. The distillery uses two small traditional-style pot stills and sources its grain both locally and abroad. Fermentation time at the distillery is unusually long and takes place over the course of five days. The current range includes a peated and unpeated five-year-old, American oak eight-year-old, French oak eight-year-old, Sherry Cask 12-year-old, and a rye whiskey, all of which are sold under the name Millstone.

Millstone 100 Rye

Made using 100 percent rye and aged for 100 months, this is a bold, spicy rye giving any American rye whiskey a run for its money.

⁕ ABV: 50% ⁕ Type: Rye ⁕ Country: Netherlands

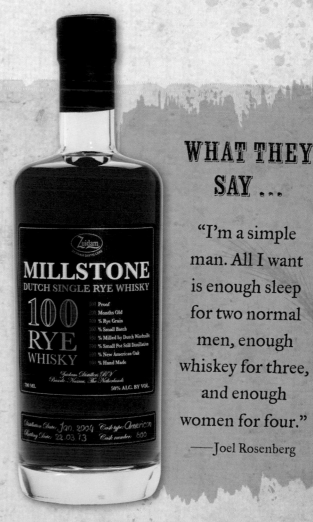

WHAT THEY SAY ...

"I'm a simple man. All I want is enough sleep for two normal men, enough whiskey for three, and enough women for four."

——Joel Rosenberg

The Whisky Castle

The Whisky Castle distillery was set up in 2002 by cheese-maker-turned-distiller Ruedi Käser. The first whiskey made it to market in 2005 as a single malt under the name Castle Hill. In the years since then the range has grown and currently contains no fewer than ten different expressions: quite a feat for a distillery that produces under 5,300 gallons (20,000 liters) of spirit a year. Among its many releases are some unique offerings, notably the Castle Hill Doublewood. This whiskey has been partially aged in chestnut casks, an oddity in whiskey production as chestnut casks are forbidden by most governing bodies of whiskey in most major areas of production and sale, and are consequently rarely found in any spirit category.

Castle Hill Doublewood

A smoked spirit aged in ex-Scotch casks and chestnut casks; the resulting whiskey is sweet and smoky, with plenty of woody spice.

★ ABV: 43% ★ TYPE: Single Malt ★ COUNTRY: Switzerland

WHAT THEY SAY …

"As they say around the Texas Legislature, if you can't drink their whiskey … take their money, and vote against 'em anyway, you don't belong in office".

——Molly Ivins

DYC

The DYC distillery in Segovia, Spain, was founded in 1958 and is one of Europe's largest and best-established distilleries. Unlike the other distilleries in Europe, DYC is enormous, and is capable of producing 2.1 million gallons (8 million liters) of grain whiskey and 530,000 gallons (2 million liters) of malt whiskey a year, for which it also has its own maltings on site. The distillery is currently under the ownership of Beam, but has been owned by a handful of different large spirit companies since the 1990s. The DYC range includes two blended whiskeys, a 3- and 8-year-old, a vatted malt, which combines some Scottish single malts with its own, and a ten-year-old single malt, which was released in 2009 to celebrate the 50th anniversary of the distillery.

DYC

A simple blended whiskey that is best used in long drinks or cocktails. A light whiskey with very little aroma and body, hints of vanilla and oak dwell in the background.

★ ABV: 40% ★ TYPE: Blended ★ COUNTRY: Spain

Warenghem

The Warenghem distillery was founded in 1900 and has been making various fruit spirits for over 100 years. The distillery has always been a family-run concern, initially belonging to the Warenghem family until 1967, when it passed to the Leizour family. It was also in this year that the distillery moved from the center to the outskirts of Lannion. The move allowed the distillery to grow and gave better access to a new water source. It wasn't until the 1980s that the distillery started to make whiskey, and in 1987 the first single malt whiskey to be distilled in France was released. The current range includes three blended whiskeys, namely Breizh Whisky, Galleg, and WB-Breton, and four single malts—Double Maturation, Classic, Sherry Finish, and Original Edition—all under the name Armorik.

Armorik Double Maturation

Aged in both French oak and sherry casks, the whiskey is full and fruity, with notes of apple and citrus.

* ABV: 46%
* TYPE: Single Malt
* COUNTRY: France

Glann ar Mor

The Glann ar Mor distillery is based on the northern coast of the Presqu'ile Sauvage (Wild Peninsula) in Larmour Pleubian, France. It's very much a coastal distillery and the name is Breton for "By the Sea." Owner Jean Donnay began his journey into whiskey-making in 1999 and has been tweaking and perfecting his whiskey for years. Regular production commenced in 2005, and in more recent years demand for the whiskey has outstripped supply. Glann ar Mor honors very traditional whiskey-making methods using wooden washbacks, direct-fired stills, and worm tubs. This in theory makes the distillery closer to an older style than any operating in Scotland today, where direct-fired stills are now extinct and worm tub condensers are a rarity. Both peated and unpeated spirits are made at Glann ar Mor, with the peated whiskey sold under the name Kornog.

Kornog Peated Single Malt

Incredibly smoky, with a clean, fresh feel followed by notes of charred bell peppers and creamy honey.

* ABV: 46% * TYPE: Single Malt * COUNTRY: France

Teerenpeli

Teerenpeli distillery in Lahti, Finland, was founded in 2002 as part of a string of restaurants, and located in the cellar under the Restaurant Taivaanranta. The whiskey first became available in 2005, but only through the restaurants as a three-year-old and later a six-year-old. It wasn't until 2011 that the whiskey became available outside of Finland as an eight-year-old. The distillery uses Finnish malted barley, which has been lightly peated, and a combination of bourbon and sherry casks for maturation. Teerenpeli has received high praise from many whiskey experts and is likened to some of the west coast Scottish single malts of old. This high praise has helped the whiskey establish itself, and in future years expansion and greater production are predicted. The distillery currently produces around 4,000 gallons (15,000 liters) a year, placing it firmly within a craft/microdistiller category. The most recent release was a 100 percent sherry-matured expression called Kaski.

8-Year-Old

Aged in bourbon and sherry casks and with an assertive quality with traces of honey, vanilla, citrus, earthy green notes, and a hint of peat.

✶ ABV: 43% ✶ Type: Single Malt ✶ Country: Finland

Braunstein

The Braunstein brewery and distillery was founded in 2005 by two whiskey enthusiasts and upon its completion became Denmark's first micro/craft distiller. The distillery makes both peated and unpeated whiskey using barley from different sources. Around 40 percent is grown domestically, whereas the rest is imported. The peated whiskey is made using malt brought in from the Port Ellen maltings on Islay, and the unpeated is supplemented by malt from Simpsons maltings, based in England. The importing of peated malt is common practice in distilling, being an enormous time and cost saver for any distillery. The first release from Braunstein, and Denmark's first single malt whiskey, was released in 2010 and was a three-year-old sherry-casked bottling called Edition No. 1. Since the first release Braunstein has added a number of other editions to its range and also created a new series called the Library Collection.

Library Collection 13:2

A lively young peated expression aged in ex-bourbon casks with smoke, ash, vanilla, and subtle citrus notes.

✶ ABV: 46% ✶ Type: Single Malt ✶ Country: Denmark

Mackmyra

In 1999 Sweden's first distillery was founded in the small town of Valbo. The distillery is undoubtedly one of Europe's most successful whiskey distilleries and is held in regard by specialists the world over. The future for Mackmyra is looking bright, as in 2012 a brand new distillery was built to help meet the rising demand. The new distillery is very advanced and is currently the tallest malt whiskey distillery in the world. There are two main types of whiskey made at Mackmyra, the first is completely smoke-free, whereas the second uses malt that has been kilned with juniper wood and bog moss. This unusual smoke source creates a unique smoky style. Since the first releases of Mackmyra in 2006–07 the distillery has issued a plethora of different releases at varying strengths and from many cask varieties.

Brukswhisky

Incredibly light and fresh, bursting with fruity flavors, with notes of vanilla and a trace of smoke.

* ABV: 41.4% * Type: Single Malt
* Country: Sweden

WHAT THEY SAY ...

"The water was not fit to drink. To make it palatable, we had to add whisky. By diligent effort, I learnt to like it".

—Sir Winston Churchill

Northern spirit

With its name, you might be forgiven for thinking Mackmyra is an archetypal Scotch, but it is actually as Swedish as Abba and Volvo. The poster child for emerging whiskey producers has a creation story that started when a group of students on a skiing vacation decided to make their own version of Scotch malt.

That was in 1998, and after trying out 170 recipes they opted for two and started making spirit in 2002. Located in an old mill in the village of Mackmyra, the distillery's first limited-edition single malt whiskey, Preludium 01, was released in February 2006. In 2010 the company launched Brukswhisky as a premium whiskey.

Mackmyra's production process emphasizes local ingredients and a natural approach. Water is filtered naturally and the whiskey is bottled from virgin or first-fill casks without color or additives.

Barrel sales have been an important part of the company's business model. It has around 10,000 owners of 8-gallon (30-liter) barrels, of whom about 2,800 also hold Mackmyra shares.

A new eco-friendly distillery was built in 2011, with the proceeds of a company flotation, to quadruple capacity from around 600,000 bottles. The seven-story building uses gravity to power many internal processes, cutting energy costs.

Mackmyra's success has inspired a new generation of Swedish whiskey makers, including Wanborga, Spirit of Hven, and Box Distillery.

SOUTH AFRICA

As a wine-producing country, it's not surprising that brandy is the favored spirit in South Africa; however, whiskey comes a strong second.

According to a report by consultancy DNA Economics, "Compared to other international markets, South Africa displays disproportionately high consumption of premium and super-premium whiskey." In other words, South Africans prefer the good stuff.

Whiskey consumption was up by nine percent between 2010–11, according to researcher South African Wine Industry Information & Systems. The drink now accounts for six percent of all alcohol consumed—the highest since the mid-1990s.

Traditionally, that has been good news for Scotch whisky, with brands such as Bell's and J&B being the tipples of choice. However, imports are suffering at the hands of local production, with Distell, South Africa's largest producer, claiming that its strongest growth in spirits comes from whiskey and Cognac.

The company blends Scottish malts and South African whiskey for its Harrier and Knights brands, and it has seen great success with two of its other homegrown brands. Three Ships, from the James Sedgwick distillery, has won international accolades, including the title of World's Best Blended Whisky at the 2012 World Whiskies Awards in London.

> The drink now accounts for six percent of all alcohol consumed, the highest since the mid-1990s.

Plaudits have also been heaped on Bain's Cape Mountain Whisky, which won Gold in the 2012 and 2013 International Wine & Spirit Competition in London. It was launched in 2009 and is also produced by James Sedgwick, which makes malt and grain whiskey on the same site.

Encouraged by the response to local whiskey, other new entrants are emerging. Drayman's is a Pretoria-based craft brewer that has turned its attention to liquor. A *solera* whiskey is already available, and a single malt is currently maturing.

James Sedgwick

The James Sedgwick Distillery is to be found in the Western Cape in the small town of Wellington, around 45 minutes from Cape Town. The distillery takes its name from Captain James Sedgwick, who arrived in South Africa in 1850 and established a successful business as a purveyor of quality liquor, tobacco, and cigars. In 1886 James Sedgwick & Co. bought the distillery, which had already been producing brandy. Today it is a modern state-of-the-art operation and is capable of producing both malt and grain whiskey.

The distillery is best known for making the popular blended whiskey Three Ships, but in 2006 it released the first single malt whiskey from South Africa. Bain's Cape Mountain Whisky is the only single grain whiskey from South Africa. It's aged for a minimum of five years and goes through an unusual double maturation process. The spirit is aged for the first three years in first-fill bourbon casks, then removed, vatted, and then reracked into first-fill bourbon casks again.

The current range of whiskeys available from the James Sedgwick distillery consists of Three Ships Select, 5-Year-Old Premium Select, Bourbon Cask Finish, and a 10-year-old single malt. The Three Ships range was joined by Bain's in 2009.

Bain's Cape Mountain Whisky

A great example of grain whiskey, with notes of toffee, vanilla, and maple syrup, vanilla custard and spicy stewed fruit.

★ ABV: 43% ★ TYPE: Single Grain

Three Ships Single Malt, 10-Year-Old

A sweet whiskey with honey and toffee on the nose and plenty of vanilla and oaky spice on the palate and finish.

★ ABV: 43% ★ TYPE: Single Malt

INDIA AND THE FAR EAST

Scotch whisky manufacturers cast an envious eye over the Indian market. It is one of the fastest growing markets for spirits in the world, but one they have limited success in reaching because of high import duties.

With imported whiskeys out of reach for many, people turn to locally produced "whiskeys." Spirits have been distilled in India since the days of British rule, but in fact many today are closer to being rums, consisting of a relatively small amount of malt whiskey. Much of the whiskey produced is molasses-based.

As well as being a potential goldmine, the Indian market is also a headache for the Scotch whisky

industry because of the manner in which producers play fast and loose with their descriptions of "whisky" and "Scotch." The Scotch Whisky Association, the zealous guardian of Scotch's global reputation, had 100 trademark oppositions and several legal cases under way in India in 2012, according to its legal report for that year.

Although the bulk of Indian whiskey is for local production, there are signs that a few producers are looking farther afield with more finessed offerings. Bangalore-based Amrut Fusion has gained a wider appreciation after scoring highly with critics.

Meanwhile John Distilleries, the sixth-largest

> With imported whiskeys out of reach for many, people turn to locally produced "whiskeys."

distiller in the world, released Paul John in 2012 to a pleasantly surprised world. The Goa-based company has produced two expressions: Edited and Brilliance.

Beyond India, Taiwan is an emerging force in whiskey manufacture. Kavalan is produced by the spirits arm of the King Car industrial group, which has interests in beverages, food, biotechnology, and aquaculture, among others. The first bottle of Kavalan was released in December 2008 and exports started in 2012. The Taiwanese are big whiskey lovers and the Kavalan distillery is a multimillion investment with a visitor center that welcomes one million enthusiasts a year. The fledgling operation is also on the doorstep of China, one of the world's emerging whiskey markets.

Amrut

The Amrut distillery in Bangalore first started making malt whiskey in the 1980s but did not release a single malt until 2004. Its first market was the United Kingdom, where the brand worked hard to establish itself. Now Amrut can be found in around 20 countries, most recently the United States, and is continuing to grow. Interestingly it was not until 2010 that the whiskey was made available in India, and it's currently only sold in the distillery's home city of Bangalore.

Amrut uses mostly domestically grown barley, sourced from the north of India and malted in Jaipur and Delhi before being moved to the distillery in Bangalore. This domestic malt is supplemented by some peated malt that is sourced from Scotland. Bangalore has an average temperature of 86°F, making it a very different climate for maturation than more traditional whiskey-making countries. The heat makes for a high angel's share, of around 10–16 percent a year, which makes the whiskey age in a very different way to whiskey in colder climes, essentially maturing more quickly, as interaction between oak and spirit is intensified by the heat.

The Amrut range is extensive, and has grown significantly in recent years, with some interesting limited releases. The core range includes a peated and unpeated 46 percent, a cask-strength peated and unpeated, and Fusion, which uses 25 percent peated malt and 75 percent unpeated. Limited releases have included Two Continents, for which casks of maturing whiskey were moved to Scotland for a final period of maturation; Kadhambam, a peated Amrut matured in ex-Oloroso casks, ex-Bangalore Blue Brandy casks and then finished off in ex-rum casks; and most recently Greedy Angels, the oldest release to date, bottled at eight years old from two casks yielding only 144 bottles.

Unpeated

A lively whiskey with a bold, spicy character and notes of honey, toffee, licorice, and oaky spice.

★ ABV: 46% ★ Type: Single Malt
★ Country: India

Amrut Fusion

A complex whiskey and winner of multiple awards. Soft smoke and spice on the nose, with dried fruit and chocolate flavors on the palate, leading to a firm peaty finish.

★ ABV: 50% ★ Type: Single Malt
★ Country: India

Paul John

Paul John Distillers was set up in 1992, and since its inception has grown to be one of the largest liquor producers in India. The company is best known in India for producing the well-known brand Original Choice, which sits comfortably in the top ten best-selling whiskeys in the world. The majority of this is sold domestically, proving beyond doubt that India is one of the most significant markets for whiskey in the world. In October 2012 the company released its first single malt, and, like Amrut, launched in the United Kingdom. The brand has been well received and has grown rapidly, now being available in several European countries. The Paul John whiskey is made in Goa using traditional methods and copper pot still distillation. Barley is sourced from north India, and some of it is peated using Scottish peat, allowing the distillery to make two totally different styles of whiskey.

The whiskey is named after the company's chairman, Paul John, who set about building the Goa distillery in 2005 with a view to making a world-class whiskey. Maturation takes place mainly in first-fill ex-bourbon casks from Kentucky. Like any whiskey matured in hot climes, Paul John has a much higher angel's share, with casks losing around ten percent each year in evaporation. This high angel's share, combined with the active casks, creates a rapid maturation effect and creates a full-flavored spirit far more quickly than in Scotland or Japan. The core range consists of two whiskeys called Edited (lightly peated) and Brilliance. Both are natural color, non-chill-filtered and bottled at 46 percent. These are supplemented by a handful of single-cask, cask-strength expressions.

Edited

Deep and spicy, with notes of mint chocolate, vanilla ice cream, toffee, spicy stewed fruit, and a trace of smoke.

★ ABV: 46% ★ Type: Single Malt ★ Country: India

Brilliance

A lively whiskey with notes of ripe fruit, toffee, marmalade, golden raisins, spicy oak, and vanilla.

★ ABV: 46% ★ Type: Single Malt ★ Country: India

Kavalan Solist Vinho

Aged in designer casks of American oak seasoned with red and white wine. Intense fruit and spice with vanilla, dark chocolate, and citrus notes.

★ ABV: 58.4%
★ TYPE: Single Malt
★ COUNTRY: Taiwan

Kavalan Classic

An incredibly soft whiskey with a sweet nose and notes of tropical fruit and honey, pear, and oaky spice on the palate and finish.

★ ABV: 40%
★ TYPE: Single Malt
★ COUNTRY: Taiwan

Kavalan

The Yuan Shan distillery was founded in 2005 and on its completion became Taiwan's first whiskey distillery. The distillery is one of the fastest built ever, with construction taking only eight months, and it lies in the northeastern part of the country, in Yilan County. Since its opening the distillery has become a major tourist attraction, with a state-of-the-art visitor center that receives a staggering one million visitors a year. That's more visitors than all of Scotland's distilleries combined. Production mirrors Scottish methods, using traditional copper pot stills and malted barley imported from Scotland. Mainly ex-bourbon casks are used for maturation, but sherry, port, and wine casks are also filled. Maturation takes place on site, with the casks being tied together in fours to minimize damage in the event of an earthquake.

The high levels of heat in Taiwan drive a rapid maturation effect and probably the highest angel's share of any distillery in the world. Around 15 percent is lost from maturing casks each year, which means the whiskey cannot be left to mature for long periods of time. The brand name for the whiskey derives from the earliest tribe that inhabited the region.

Kavalan's main market is China, but since its first release in 2008 the brand has grown rapidly and is available in over 20 different countries. The current range consists of Kavalan Classic, Concertmaster, Podium, and Fino Sherry Cask. These are supplemented by the Solist collection, featuring some of the distillery's best releases from various cask types bottled at cask strength, including ex-bourbon. There is also a limited release called King Car Conductor.

AUSTRALIA AND NEW ZEALAND

Although there is no record of the first distilleries in Australia, it seems likely that the colony was producing hard liquor soon after the arrival of European settlers in 1788. At any rate, by 1796 governor John Hunter was complaining of the widespread existence of "illicit distilleries of spirituous liquors."

As the distilling industry became established during the nineteenth century, distillers favored rum and gin over whiskey, which tended to be imported. There were attempts at creating an Australian dram, notably Corio, but it is not fondly remembered, earning the description "gut rot." It ceased production in 1989.

Around that time a new generation of Australian whiskey-makers came to the fore. Led by Tasmania's Bill Lark, they focused on quality over quantity. Lark decided that conditions on the island were perfect for whiskey-making, and set about overturning Tasmania's century-and-a-half-long ban on distilling. Today Lark Single Malt is one of around ten whiskeys produced in Tasmania.

Overall, there are more than 20 active whiskey distilleries in Australia, producing a range of styles. Many are bottled at cask strength and are typically non-chill-filtered. Sullivan's Cove has received accolades as one of the world's best whiskeys, and

Overall, there are more than 20 active whiskey distilleries in Australia, producing a range of styles.

the Nant Distillery was rated as the maker of one of the top 50 whiskeys in the world.

Neighboring New Zealand has also caught the whiskey bug, which is perhaps not surprising, given its purported similarities in climate and terrain to Scotland. Early distilling seems to have been initiated by Scottish settlers in 1838, and thrived

particularly in the Dunedin and Otago region until the government cracked down in the 1870s.

After many years of imports, today's whiskeys are relatively small-scale, from distillers such as Kaiapoi, which produces a 13-year-old malt, and Hokonoi, whose single malt, the Coaster, uses driftwood and seaweed to malt barley.

Hellyers Road

The Hellyers Road distillery was set up in 1997 and is Australia's largest boutique distillery, making around 26,500 gallons (100,000 liters) of spirit a year. The distillery sources Tasmanian barley, which is malted at the Cascade Brewery in Hobart, some of which is dried with peat imported from Scotland. The malt is then transported to the distillery for mashing and fermentation.

An unusual quirk of Hellyers is that the pots on its pot stills are made from stainless steel, while the heads, necks, and lyne arms are made of copper. Mainly ex-bourbon casks are used for maturation, but some ex-Tasmanian wine casks are filled. The range has six expressions: Original, Roaring Forty, ten-year-old, Peated, Slightly Peated, and Pinot Noir finish.

Roaring Forty

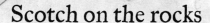

Sweet cereal notes and traces of fruit on the nose, with chocolate orange and vanilla on the palate and with licorice and a trace of coffee beans on the finish.

✴ ABV: 40% ✴ Type: Single Malt ✴ Country: Australia

Scotch on the rocks

New Zealand may only have a fledgling whiskey industry compared to neighboring Australia, but the "land of the long white cloud" played a crucial role in one of the most intriguing whiskey tales of recent years.

In January 2010 the New Zealand Antarctic Heritage Trust excavated five crates of Scotch whisky and brandy from beneath Sir Ernest Shackleton's 1908 base in Antarctica. The intrepid explorer had taken 46 crates of Mackinlay's Rare Old Highland Malt with him on the British Antarctic Expedition.

One crate of whisky was removed from the base to Canterbury Museum and carefully thawed. Three bottles from the crate were then returned to Scotland on the personal jet of Whyte & Mackay owner Dr. Vijay Mallya. Whyte & Mackay master blender Richard Paterson subsequently spent eight weeks reproducing a whisky of more than 100 years old for which no recipe existed.

Described as elegant and refined, with pear and fruit flavors and a hint of smoke, the whisky recreates the original from Glen Mhor distillery. Fifty thousand bottles went on sale the following year, with five percent of the £100 ($160) price going to the New Zealand Heritage Trust, which found and uncovered the original bottles. The donation will help to maintain Shackleton's historic base.

In January 2013 New Zealand Prime Minister John Key returned the three bottles to the trust in Antarctica. The bottles were then conserved and returned to Shackleton's camp at Cape Royds.

Sullivans Cove

Sullivans Cove whiskey began in 1994 in Cambridge, near the city of Hobart. The distillery's production has been fitful since it started, with three periods of activity under different owners. The latest owner has done a fantastic job in getting its whiskey out to a wider audience, and along the way has spread the word about Tasmanian whiskey. The distillery buys in its wash from the nearby and long-established Cascade Brewery, which it then transports to the distillery for distillation. The distillery operates a single pot still, which is an oddity in the world of modern whiskey production, where stills usually work in pairs: a wash still and a spirit still. After distillation the spirit is filled into casks made of American and French oak for maturation. Unlike other distilleries where casks are then married together in an attempt to create a uniform whiskey, the Sullivan's team bottles almost every cask individually. In this way, subtle differences can occur between bottlings. The current range from Sullivan's Cove consists of three whiskeys, the Double Cask, American Oak Bourbon Cask, and French Oak Port Cask. The Double Cask is the only release in which any casks are married, and for each batch two bourbon casks are brought together with one French Oak port cask, all of which have been matured for ten years.

American Oak Bourbon Cask

Sweet and creamy on the nose, with vanilla and lemon loaf cake on the palate leading to a long, spicy finish.

★ ABV: 47.5% ★ Type: Single Malt
★ Country: Tasmania

Double Cask

Floral notes combine with vanilla and oaky spice on the nose, with honeycomb, hard candy and chocolate notes on the palate.

★ ABV: 40% ★ Type: Single Malt
★ Country: Tasmania

WHAT THEY SAY ...

"Come, let me know what it is that makes a Scotch man happy!"

—Samuel Johnson

Overeem

The Old Hobart distillery (home of Overeem whiskey) was founded in 2005 by Casey Overeem but didn't start producing spirit until two years later in 2007. In the years prior to founding the distillery, Casey spent a huge amount of time researching spirit production in Norway and Scotland, and, inspired by some Norwegian relatives, began experimenting with different stills and production methods. Mashing and fermentation takes place off-site, in this case at the neighboring Lark Distillery, where Overeem has two designated washbacks. This allows control of fermentation and use of the firm's own strains of yeast.

The Lark Distillery has been instrumental in a number of Tasmania's distilleries, and is currently set to acquire Old Hobart. Indeed, without the efforts of Bill Lark (founder of Lark), there might well be no distilleries in Tasmania at all. Bill, among others, lobbied the government to overturn a distilling ban that had been in place in Tasmania since 1838. Since the law was overturned, many new distilleries have popped up, reviving what was once an established distilling industry. Many distilleries in Tasmania work with neighboring distilleries for mutual benefit and financial gain. This is unique and certainly not something you see in countries where distilleries are owned by big companies. After fermentation at Lark, the wash is transported back to Overeem, where distillation begins. Spirit is filled into three types of cask: ex-bourbon, ex-sherry, and ex-port. The current range consists of four whiskeys, two from sherry casks and two from port casks, with one of each being bottled at 43 percent and 60 percent.

Overeem Port Cask

Chocolate, orange peel, and clove on the nose with deep, spicy fruity flavors on the palate, and chocolate-covered raisins on the finish.

✦ ABV: 60% ✦ Type: Single Malt ✦ Country: Tasmania

Overeem Sherry Cask

Fruitcake and gummy candies on the nose, with raisin and nut chocolate on the palate and cocoa and oaky spice on the finish.

✦ ABV: 60% ✦ Type: Single Malt ✦ Country: Tasmania

New World Whisky

Starward hails from the New World Whisky Distillery in Melbourne. The distillery is located in an old Qantas maintenance hangar at Essendon Fields, which was once Melbourne's airport, and was set up by David Vitale, previously of Lark distillery.

The whiskey hasn't been around long, with the distillery being founded in 2008, and its first release in 2013. Maturation takes place in 13-, 26-, and 52-gallon (50-, 100-, and 200- liter) casks that have been seasoned with Australian fortified wine prior to being filled at the distillery. One major advantage in using smaller casks is that the whiskey matures at a more rapid rate, as the wood-to-whiskey ratio is much higher. Just the one whiskey is available so far and is sold under the name Starward.

Starward

A light, lively whiskey with a big, fruity character. Notes of toasty oak, caramel, and vanilla mingle with dried and ripe fruit flavors.

✶ ABV: 43% ✶ Type: Single Malt ✶ Country: Australia

The New Zealand Whisky Company/ Willowbank Distillery

In 1974 the Willowbank Distillery at Dunedin was opened and began production of malt whiskeys such as Wilson's and 45 South. Following its sale to Seagram the whiskey was marketed under the name Lammerlaw. Sadly, the distillery was not to last and was mothballed in 2000 by its owner, now Foster's, never to reopen, with its stills being removed and sent to Fiji to be used to make rum. The New Zealand Whisky Company formed in 2001 and purchased the remaining 600 casks from Foster's, with the long-term plan of building a distillery. The range consists of Milford Single Malt 10-, 15-, 18-, and 20-year-olds, South Island Single Malt 18- and 21-year-olds, Dunedin Doublewood (a single malt), Diggers and Ditch (a blended malt using New Zealand and Tasmanian whiskey), the Water of Leith (a ten-year-old blend), and a handful of single-cask releases from the 1980s and '90s.

Dunedin Distillery Doublewood 15-Year-Old

Aged in a combination of ex-bourbon and French oak casks. Creamy and soft, with notes of dried fruit and nuts, toffee, and vanilla.

✶ ABV: 40% ✶ Type: Single Malt ✶ Country: New Zealand

GLOSSARY OF TERMS

ABV—alcohol by volume.

Aging/maturation—the period during which the whiskey is kept in oak barrels. The process stops once the whiskey is bottled.

Age statement—the age of the whiskey as specified on the label (see **NAS**).

Angel's share—the part of the maturing spirit that evaporates during maturation, usually around 2 percent a year in Scotland.

Blended whiskey—whiskey made using a mix of malt whiskeys and grain whiskeys.

Cask strength—whiskey bottled straight from the cask without diluting with water and therefore stronger.

Charring—the insides of bourbon barrels used to store most whiskey in the world are often burned/charred to enhance the interaction between the spirit and the oak.

Chill-filtering—a process in which matured whiskey is chilled to between 39°F and 14°F and then filtered to remove naturally occurring lipids in the whiskey before bottling. This process prevents the whiskey becoming cloudy when chilled or when diluted to below 46 percent.

Classic Malts Selection—a collection of six single malt whiskies, launched and marketed in 1988 by United Distillers and Vintners (now Diageo).

Column still system/Coffey Patent still—a modern method of spirit production, which allows for quick and efficient continuous distillation and the mass production of grain whiskey as well as other spirits.

Cooper/cooperage—maker of barrels/premises for making barrels.

Distilling—process by which the wash is turned into spirit.

Dram—Scottish term for a measure of whiskey, approximately one eighth of an ounce.

Expressions – different versions of whisky released by a distillery, often identified by an age statement or a finish.

Grain whiskey—whiskey made using a mash of various grains (corn, wheat, barley) and distilled using column stills.

Grist—ground dried malt.

Independent bottlings – whisky bought in bulk from distilleries who solely distil for blending purposes, sold by independent bottlers under their own name, but with the original whisky identified.

Kilning—stage during which the germinating barley is dried.

Lincoln County Process—required for Tennessee whiskey, a process in which the whiskey is filtered through a bed of maple charcoal.

Lomond still—short, squat type of still, developed in the 1950s in order to create different spirit styles from one still.

Low wines—liquid after first distillation.

Lyne arms—angled pipes from the top of the still to the condenser.

Malt—barley that has been germinated and dried.

Malting—the process in which the barley is soaked in water and left to germinate.

Mashing—the process in which dried ground barley (grist) is mixed with hot water.

Mash bill—grains that have been mixed and blended before fermentation.

Mash tun—vessel for mashing.

Mouthfeel—a tasting term used to describe whiskey in terms not covered by taste and smell, such as its tactile qualities.

NAS—no age statement.

New-make spirit—the new spirit collected from the middle cut of the final distillation.

Peat—natural bog fuel used to dry barley and to impart flavor.

Pot still (or still)—pear-shaped copper kettle used for distillation.

PPM—part per million (of phenols). Measure of peatiness.

Proof—amount of alcohol by volume.

Single malt—malt whiskey from one distillery only.

Scotch—whisky that has been distilled, matured for three years in oak casks, and bottled in Scotland.

Sour mash—a step in production where part of the unwanted distillate is added to the mash or the wash, or both, in order to help control the PH levels and aid in flavor development and consistency in the final product.

Spirit receiver—the final holding point for the new-make spirit.

Spirit safe—receptacle into which the spirit is fed after passing through the stills.

Vatted/blended malt—a type of whiskey in which two or more malt whiskeys are "vatted" or blended together.

Vatting—the process of mixing different whiskeys.

Wash—the alcoholic liquid produced by adding yeast to the wort.

Wash back—tank where the wort has yeast added and ferments, becoming wash.

Wash still—the still used for the first stage of distilling.

Wood finishing—when the whiskey is transferred from the cask where it was first matured for a second maturation, often to a cask of different wood for additional flavor.

Worm/worm tub—a long, coiled copper tube, attached to the lyne arm of the pot still, and fitted into a large wooden vat filled with cold water to condense the spirit vapor.

Wort—a sugary liquid made from grist mixed with hot water in a mash tun.

INDEX OF WHISKEYS

We would like to thank all the featured distilleries for supplying the bulk of the photographs used in this book—in particular Frances Drury at Diageo, Elisabeth Trolle, Dan Cohen at Beam Global, Alison Hall at Heaven Hill and Amy Preske at Buffalo Trace—and Henrietta Drane for her dedication and hard work.

Adnams 197 • Amrut 209, 210 • Angus Dundee 23, 47, 62 • Ardbeg 76 • Ardmore 56 • Arran 18, 88, 89 • Bailie Nicol Jarvie 103 • Bain's 190 • Balvenie 25 • Beam Inc. 85, 122, 128, 129, 134, 136, 148, 149, 172 • Ben Nevis 56 • BenRiach 26, 27 • Benrinnes 24 • Benromach 28 • Bernheim 16 • Big Peat 116 • Black Bottle 103 • Bladnoch 48, 49, 52 • Blantons 142 • Blue Hangar 116 • Braunstein 6, 7, 8, 9, 10, 11, 13, 15, 194, 195, 202 • Brown-Forman Corporation 7, 139, 153, 154, 155, 158, 159 • Bruichladdich 18, 19, 78, 79 • Buffalo Trace 142 • Bunnahabhain 8, 19, 80 • Cameron Brig 120 • Caribou Crossing 173 • Chichibu 182 • Compass Box 117 • Copper Fox 169 • Corsair 156 • Cutty Sark 4, 5, 101, 105 • Devil's Share 162 • Dewar's 106 • Diageo 6, 7, 12, 13, 20, 21, 29, 30, 40, 44, 45, 49, 53, 54, 55, 58, 59, 61, 69, 72, 81, 84, 86, 87, 92, 106, 111, 112, 113, 114, 123, 126, 127, 136, 143, 157, 173, 176 • Dry Fly 162 • DYC 200 • Eagle Rare 143 • Elijah Craig 144 • Evan Williams 144 • Famous Grous 107 • FEW 14, 15, 161, 163 • Forty Creek 174, 175 • Four Roses 137, 145 • George T Stagg 145 • Georgia Moon 146 • Getty Images 70, 71, 104, 130, 167, 181, 183, 186, 187, 189, 216 • Gibson 174 • Girvan 120 • Glann ar Mor 201 • Glen Grant 36 • Glen Moray 28, 68 • Glen Scotia 96 • GlenDronach 31 • Glenfarclas 32, 33 • Glenfiddich 16, 17, 34, 35 • Glengoyne 55, 64, 65 • Glengyle 96, 97 • Glenlossie 36 • Glenmorangie 66, 67 • Glenrothes 38, 39 • Grants 100, 101, 108, 109 • Graphicstock 19 • Heaven Hill 15, 136, 137, 141, 146, 147 • Hellyer's Road 216 • High West 163 • Highland Park 87, 90, 91 • Hudsons 164, 165 • Inver House Distillers Ltd 57, 68, 71, 110 • Invergordon 121 • Isle of Skye 110 • James Sedgwick 205, 206, 207 • Jameson 122 • Kavalan 190, 212, 213 • Kilchoman 10, 82, 83 • Larceny 149 • Macallan 42, 43 • Mackmyra 203 • Mellow Corn 150 • Monkey Shoulder 119 • Morrison Bowmore Distillers Ltd 50, 63, 77 • Nikka Whisky Distilling Co. 187, 189 • Noah's Mill 150 • Old Hobart 193, 218 • Park Hyatt, Tokyo 182 • Paul John 211 • Penderyn 197 • Pernod Ricard 24, 37, 41, 46, 47, 89, 102, 104, 129, 131, 133, 135, 172, 177 • Rittenhouse 151 • Rock Town 166 • Sazerac 151, 152 • Shutterstock 13, 37, 41, 51, 57, 60, 74, 75, 85, 94, 95, 121, 122, 123, 124, 125, 128, 132, 138, 140, 141, 153, 160, 161, 169, 170, 171, 178, 179, 180, 181, 190, 191, 192, 193, 204, 205, 208, 209, 214, 215, 220, 221, 222, 223, 224 • Slyrs 198 • Smooth Ambler 167 • Springbank 10, 20, 95, 98, 99, 221 • St George 196 • Still Waters 138, 176 • Stranahan's 168 • Sullivan's Cove 217 • Suntory 178, 179, 180, 183, 184, 185, 188 • Teerenpeli 191, 202 • The Belgian Owl 192, 198 • The New Zealand Whisky Company 215, 219 • The Six Isles 119 • The Whisky Castle 200 • The Whisky Lounge 118 • Tobermory 93 • Tomatin 73 • Tullibardine 17, 72, 73 • Tweeddale 111 • W.L. Weller 152 • Waldrietler Distillery 6, 7, 12, 199 • Warenghen 195, 201 • WhistlePig 138, 171, 177 • Whyte & Mackay 46, 60, 115, 118 • Wild Turkey 153 • William Grant 22, 23 • Zuidam 199